TOWARDS A POLITICAL ECONOMY FOR AFRICA

Also by Timothy M. Shaw

AFRICA PROJECTED *(co-editor with Olajide Aluko)*

NIGERIAN FOREIGN POLICY: Alternative Perceptions and Projections *(co-editor with Olajide Aluko)*

THE POLITICAL ECONOMY OF AFRICAN FOREIGN POLICY: Comparative Analyses *(co-editor)*

AFRICA AND THE INTERNATIONAL POLITICAL SYSTEM *(co-editor)*

ALTERNATIVE FUTURES FOR AFRICA *(editor)*

ZAMBIA'S FOREIGN POLICY: Studies in Diplomacy and Dependence *(co-author)*

CANADA, SCANDINAVIA AND SOUTHERN AFRICA *(co-editor)*

CONFLICT AND CHANGE IN SOUTHERN AFRICA *(co-editor)*

THE POLITICS OF AFRICA: Dependence and Development *(co-editor)*

TOWARDS A POLITICAL ECONOMY FOR AFRICA

The Dialectics of Dependence

Timothy M. Shaw

Director, Center for African Studies, and Professor of Political Science, Dalhousie University, Nova Scotia, Canada

St. Martin's Press New York

St. Martin's Press, Inc., 175 Fifth Avenue, New York, NY 10010
Printed in Hong Kong
Published in the United Kingdom by The Macmillan Press Ltd
First published in the United States of America in 1985

ISBN 0–312–81043–1

Library of Congress Cataloging in Publication Data

Shaw, Timothy M.
Towards a political economy for Africa.

Includes bibliographical references and index.
1. Africa—Economic conditions—1960– . 2. Africa—Dependency on foreign countries. 1. Title.
HC800.S53 1984 337.6 84–8218
ISBN 0–312–81043–1

For Jane, for being

Contents

List of Tables

Preface

This long essay was designed and drafted during a sabbatical safari through Africa in the early months of 1982 and subsequent return visits to Nigeria and Ethiopia in mid-1983; it was revised and retyped during a return to my *alma mater,* the University of Sussex, in the summer of 1982 and during periodic stopovers at my 'base' university in the summer of 1983. Although its form took shape during sabbatical and subsequent visits to universities in Africa (Abidjan, Addis Ababa, Bayero, Botswana, Calabar, Dar es Salaam, Ghana, Ife, Jos, Nairobi, Port Harcourt, Sokoto, Zambia, and Zimbabwe) and North America (Boston, Harvard, Indiana, Toronto and UCLA), its genesis really dates back to two radicalising experiences on the continent: lecturing at the universities of Zambia (1973–4) and Ife (1979–80). Together these two encounters introduced me to the complexities and contradictions, dynamics and impacts of 'capitalism' in Africa, insights which traditional 'African Studies' doesn't provide.

This study is intended, then, to be both revisionist and radical, a timely enterprise, perhaps, as Africa progresses from its first twenty years of 'independence' into the final two decades of the twentieth century. The first half of the 1980s includes two symbolic sets of anniversaries for Africa. First, in 1983 the continent celebrated both a quarter-century of the Economic Commission for Africa and the first twenty years of the Organisation of African Unity, not inconsiderable achievements given the genesis of these institutions and the intervening series of conflicts which have continued to threaten them. And second, in 1984 – that symbolic year of Orwellian mystique – the continent marks the centenary of the notorious Treaty of Berlin: the basic framework for the continent's colonisation. The survival of a degree of independence and optimism despite 1884 and subsequent challenges is reason enough for celebration.

However, as this study suggests, Africa as a whole is hardly much closer to either self-reliant or self-sustaining development than it was twenty years ago; it is to be hoped that the next two decades will mark an advance in the Basic Human Needs of the *mwananachi.* But for this to occur – for autonomous and meaningful development to be realised at personal, national and continental levels – substantial shifts will have to take place in the class character of Africa's political economies. *A luta continua!*

Lusaka and Addis Ababa TIMOTHY M. SHAW

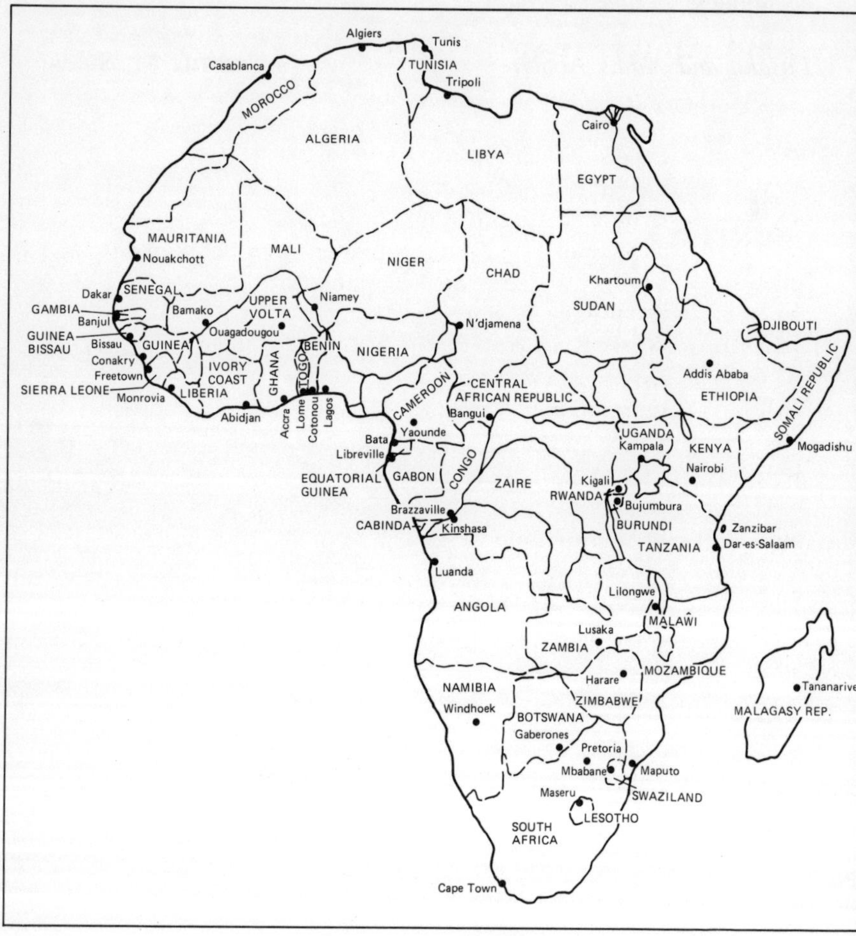
Algiers
Tunis
Casablanca
TUNISIA
Tripoli
MOROCCO
ALGERIA
LIBYA
Cairo
EGYPT
MAURITANIA
MALI
NIGER
CHAD
Nouakchott
Khartoum
SUDAN
Dakar
SENEGAL
GAMBIA
Banjul
UPPER VOLTA
Niamey
Bamako
N'djamena
DJIBOUTI
GUINEA BISSAU
Bissau
GUINEA
Ouagadougou
BENIN
Conakry
IVORY COAST
GHANA
TOGO
NIGERIA
Addis Ababa
Freetown
SIERRA LEONE
Monrovia
LIBERIA
CAMEROON
CENTRAL AFRICAN REPUBLIC
ETHIOPIA
SOMALI REPUBLIC
Abidjan
Accra
Lome
Cotonou
Lagos
Bangui
Bata
Yaounde
UGANDA
Kampala
KENYA
Mogadishu
Libreville
Nairobi
EQUATORIAL GUINEA
GABON
CONGO
ZAIRE
Kigali
RWANDA
Bujumbura
Brazzaville
BURUNDI
CABINDA
Kinshasa
Zanzibar
Dar-es-Salaam
TANZANIA
Luanda
Lilongwe
ANGOLA
MALAŴI
Lusaka
ZAMBIA
Harare
MOZAMBIQUE
NAMIBIA
Tananarive
ZIMBABWE
Windhoek
BOTSWANA
MALAGASY REP.
Gaberones
Pretoria
Mbabane
Maputo
Maseru
SWAZILAND
LESOTHO
SOUTH AFRICA
Cape Town

List of Abbreviations

BHN	Basic Human Needs
EAC	East African Community
ECA	Economic Commission for Africa
ECOWAS	Economic Community of West African States
EEC	European Economic Community
FLS	Front Line States
IBRD	World Bank (International Bank for Reconstruction and Development)
IMF	International Monetary Fund
NICs	Newly Industrialising Countries
NIEO	New International Economic Order
OAU	Organisation of African Unity
OECD	Organisation for Economic Co-operation and Development
SADCC	Southern African Development Co-ordination Conference
UN	United Nations

Introduction: The African Condition[1]

> 'The continent itself seems to be well endowed with resources but a disproportionate number of people in the population of the continent is undernourished and underprivileged.
>
> Africa is the most centrally located of all the continents, but politically it is perhaps the most marginal. This anomaly has implications for *Pax Africana.*'—Ali A. Mazrui, *The African Condition: A Political Diagnosis* (London: Heinemann, 1980) pp. 72 and 116.

> 'What comes out of Africa is neither new, nor exciting, nor seeming likely to be such, but what is old, predictable and boring. The liberating nationalism of twenty and thirty years ago was nearly always a joyful lift to the spirit . . . the formative experience of Africa's under-30s [is] one of deepening crisis apparently beyond cure by any familiar remedy . . . More and more often, from all I hear, there is a new consciousness of choice . . . that Africa must revolutionise itself and soon; or go, and sooner, entirely to the devil.'—Basil Davidson 'Beyond the Flags and Anthems', *New Statesman,* 24 March 1978, pp. 391–2.

> '[In] order to be a respectable Africanist, by which I mean simply a scholar whose interest, regardless of discipline, is focused on Africa, one must be a Marxist.'—Robert Martin, 'The use of state power to overcome underdevelopment', *Journal of Modern African Studies,* 18(2), June 1980, p. 315.

Africa is at an historic conjuncture as the 1980s open: the assumptions, prescriptions and projections of the first twenty years of independence are no longer valid. Instead, 'developmentalist' ideology is being replaced by 'self-reliance' as the contemporary continental motif; the elusiveness of development and the unevenness of growth have combined to force a reconsideration of strategy and scenario on Africa's statesmen and scholars. Hence this book: a preliminary analysis of Africa in the post-Bretton Woods era.

The contemporary African condition has been well expressed by the Executive Secretary of the Economic Commission for Africa (ECA), Professor Adebayo Adedeji:

> Africa more than the other third world regions, is . . . faced with a development crisis of great portent . . . If past trends persist and if there are no fundamental changes in the mix of economic policies that African governments have pursued during the last decade and a half and if the current efforts to fundamentally change the international economic system and relations fail to yield concrete positive results, the African region as a whole will be worse off compared with the rest of the world at the end of this century than it was in 1960.[2]

RECONCEPTUALISATION OF ASSUMPTIONS, PRESCRIPTIONS AND PROJECTIONS

A growing awareness of this unenviable situation has produced a re-evaluation of policies in the past, present and future at the political level – the Organisation of African Unity (OAU) system – and at the national level (both inside and outside Africa), as well as in the ECA and other parts of the United Nations (UN) Organisation. Moreover, it has confronted students of Africa with the imperative of re-examining their own forms and frameworks of analysis. In short, the current African condition – that of crisis – has produced a timely reconsideration of assumptions, prescriptions and projections.

First, analytic *assumptions* have evolved markedly away from 'political modernisation' and towards 'political economy'.[3] The widespread structural-functional and systems approaches – with their focus on inputs, outputs and feedback – have been superseded by a concern for the interface between politics and economics – focus on property, production and the proletariat. Notions of process and order have been replaced by those of contradiction and dialectic. If the mentor of the first generation of African political studies was James Coleman, that of the new generation is surely Samir Amin.[4]

Second, policy *prescriptions* have developed along with intellectual assumptions. The preoccupation with political institutions and societal specialisation has been replaced by a concentration on control over the means of production and on the relationship and distribution between different sectors and classes. If the motif of the 'modernisers' was growth – higher national product at any cost – that of the 'radicals' is development – the satisfaction of the Basic Human Needs (BHN) first. While the former advocated international incorporation as a means to expansion – exogenous orientation – the latter espouse self-reliance as the prerequisite for development – endogenous orientation. Both perspectives continue to be refined and to be used as the bases of divergent policy documents. The modernisation perspective has been revived and revised in the latest World Bank report on the continent – *Accelerated Development in sub-Saharan Africa: An Agenda for Action* – while the radical alternative has been presented most coherently in the OAU's first economic statement – *The Lagos Plan of Action.*[5]

And third, mid-term *projections* have been recalculated away from the naïve and optimistic expectations of the independence decade towards more sophisticated and pessimistic previews of the mid-seventies and beyond. It is no longer assumed – even less desired – that Africa should emulate the advanced industrialised states in terms either of economic structure or of national ideology. Rather, given the problems confronting the metropolitan countries – social and infrastructural decay, environmental pollution and declining living standards – the periphery should design its own appropriate goals, structures and procedures.

In short, while at an aggregate level the future is not bright, the very gloominess of projections might force, as Davidson's opening citation indicates, a re-evaluation of aspirations and institutions leading to alternative strategies and scenarios. Africa, as Adedeji insists, can yet achieve greater degrees of both self-reliance and self-confidence:

> [There] is a hidden psychological factor: the re-acquisition of confidence in identifying, defining and solving socio-economic problems; in social and material invention and innovation and their diffusion.[6]

This volume is intended to be one contribution to the achievement of African self-reliance and self-confidence in terms of intellectual debate as well as of developmental design. Independence did not lead to either indigenous analysis or relevant prognosis. Rather, one indicator of being at the periphery, as Mazrui's opening quote suggests, is the time-lag in both examination and execution: the countries most in need of sensitive and sophisticated advice get the worst. This is partly because of a paucity of data; but it is also partly a result of inappropriate frameworks for analysis.

TOWARDS A NEO-MARXIST ANALYSIS OF AFRICA

This exercise is but one attempt to overcome this lamentable situation: the African condition is neither unknown nor hopeless if appropriate methods are employed. Instead of repeating past errors by looking at 'nation-building' or 'political engineering', the approach advanced here is explicitly 'neo-Marxist'. The level of analysis includes substructure as well as superstructure; the methodology is materialist as well as historical; and social conflict as well as co-operation is incorporated.[7] The perspective is 'Marxist' in that, as advocated by Martin in his opening quote, it focuses on class, production and contradiction; it is 'neo-Marxist' in that it does not rest simply on a bourgeois–proletarian dichotomy, neither does it anticipate unequivocal revolutionary changes.

Rather, the *methodology* is Marxist, focusing on modes and relations of production, whereas the *theory* is non-Marxist, for no particular resolution of contradictions is anticipated. So, the viewpoint presented here is eclectic within the materialist tradition, reflective of changes within the world capitalist system on the one hand and indicative of the novelty and complexity of class formation in Africa on the other hand. In a 'post-industrial' and 'post-independence' period 'imperialism' is no longer a monolithic system, neither is Africa simply a world of ethnicity, race and religion. The imperative of going beyond simplistic Marxist formulations is well expressed by Issa Shivji:

> Those [Marxists] who argue that political independence does not bring any change in the class character of state power are hard put to analyse the politics of neo-colonialism. They have to explain the local politics as a direct, crude reflection of inter-imperialist rivalries despite having first posited a monolithic, global financial oligarchy. On the other hand, their interpretation of local political struggle and alignments is reduced to isolated conspiracies and intrigues since they deny the role of local classes in state power.[8]

Any understanding of contemporary, 'post-colonial' Africa necessitates, then, going beyond both 'dependence' and 'imperialism' and towards a more subtle and sophisticated conception of Africa in the world system.[9] Africa's leaders are neither autonomous nor robots; they reflect diverse class and fractional interests located within the continent but not separable from their extra-continental connections. In short, political economies situated in Africa respond to various internal and external demands; the balance between these varies between states and between periods. Hence the new diversity of reality, ideology and projection.

This variability requires investigation: the adoption of a comparative method by which to examine, contrast and explain. Not that we should either lose sight of common interests or revert to the static comparative typologies of yesteryear. Rather, the intent here is to advance understanding through comparisons of different social coalitions and contradictions: the dialectic is not the same everywhere, another reason for abandoning over-simplifications which characterise Africa as a homogenous dependent continent. The continent is complex rather than straightforward. As Aidan Foster-Carter suggests in his advocacy of neo-Marxism as the approach by which to understand Third World political economies:

> It is characteristic of colonial and neo-colonial situations that different modes of production, in various relations to one another, exist side by side, each generating contradictions within itself, and generating contradictions among one another. Thus ultimately, any class can only be analysed in terms of the historically specific constellation of class relations.[10]

The richness of African political economies is revealed in the commonalities and contrasts of its cultures. These reflect diverse historical relationships both between people and their environment and between owners and labourers, the exploiters and the exploited. For not all of the surplus has left the continent: Benin bronzes, Egyptian pyramids, Ethiopian churches and Zimbabwean cities reveal an ability to accumulate capital and reproduce classes. Likewise today, uneven access to surplus, especially when translated into vital foreign exchange, affects the distribution of houses, cars, videotapes and stereos. This capture of surplus varies not only over time but also among countries and among classes: the dynamic of accumulation.

The intrusion of the nationalist movement in the 1960s plus the evolution of the capitalist system in the 1970s together enhanced Africa's prospects of capturing surplus. They did not, of course, ensure it as the continued decline of certain African political economies indicates. But some bourgeois fractions in certain situations – particularly the bureaucratic bourgeoisie in state capitalist systems with strategic resources – have been able to accumulate both for themselves and for their countries: collective infrastructures as well as individual properties have expanded in, say, Ivory Coast, Kenya and Morocco. This embourgeoisement is a function of the changing dialectic in the world capitalist system which has become both more global and more hierarchical: production is international but uneven; some interests are advanced (e.g. anyone associated with the coffee windfall in Kenya or the oil boom in Nigeria), while others are relegated to historical irrelevance (e.g. owners and producers of sisal in Tanzania and cocoa in Ghana). Such a perspective on the (albeit limited) prospects for accumulation in the periphery in a post-independence, post-Bretton Woods world is of major importance for both theory and policy, as Henrik Secher Marcussen and Jens Erik Torp indicate:

> [Changes] in the international division of labour, with the consequent establishment of a profound capitalist development in some countries of the periphery, suggest that this new situation has to be understood within the framework of capitalism's global reproduction. The role of the periphery, in the context of this theory of the internationalisation of capital, cannot primarily be analysed with concepts like dependency, underdevelopment, or blocked development. Rather, capitalism's basic tendency to unequal development must be stressed, the consequences of which are both an equalisation process (where conditions of production such as technological development, wage levels, profit etc. equalise) and a differentiation process, in the centre as well as in the periphery. Capitalism's global expansion thereby causes the establishment of an international reproductive hierarchy, in which tendencies towards equalisation are constantly succeeded by new differentiation patterns, and in which these basic conceptions express themselves at the regional, national and international level.[11]

These two twin contemporary features – *internationalisation and differentiation on the one hand and, on the other hand, factionalism within and between both centre and periphery* – have profound implications for the prospects of development in Africa over the remaining two decades of this century. These features are also reinforcing and cumulative leading to divergent potentials between neighbouring African states, which in turn affect the prospects for regional and global integration: is collective self-reliance a chimera which really reflects common bourgeois interests in Africa rather than a genuine developmental direction? If dependence was a consensual and populist reaction to underdevelopment, what African policy stance will be constructed in a post-dependence, post-growth world system? New and exacerbated inequalities on the continent complicate the quest for diplomatic and developmental cohesion. They also serve to intensify intellectual curiosity and debate and hence inform *praxis* for the immediate future.

As always throughout history, times of crisis concentrate the mind and compel creativity. This is true of much of Africa in the contemporary decade: the very intensity of the depression is forcing innovation whether it be in the revival of 'traditional' forms of house-making and housekeeping in Ghana, or in the ability to 'manufacture' cars and other products out of scrap metal in Nigeria. This cultural and technological renaissance is not simply 'primitivistic', a rediscovery of long-forgotten 'roots', but is also 'modernistic': an ability to experiment and innovate in energy, medicine, construction and domestic sectors. Nevertheless, this renaissance is presently problematic and patchy, advanced by some regimes and classes but ignored or repressed by others. Yet current plans and strategies provide some basis in framework and function for such self-reliance and self-actualisation.

INCREASING INEQUALITIES WITHIN AND BETWEEN STATES

Two contemporary features of the continent in particular require attention to be able to situate the dialectic of renaissance and repression; these inequalities have not been treated in the established literatures on Africa's comparative and international politics.[12] First, inequalities *within* African political economies: independence did not herald a 'golden age' for most of Africa's people but it did advance the interests of the indigenous bourgeoisie in both the polity and the

TABLE I·1 *Basic indicators for Africa*

	Population (millions) mid-1979	Area (thousands of square kilometers)	GNP per capita: Dollars 1979	GNP per capita: Average annual growth rate (percent) 1960–79	Average annual rate of inflation (percent): 1960–70	Average annual rate of inflation (percent): 1970–79	Adult literacy (percent) 1976*	Life expectancy at birth (years) 1979	Average index of food production per capita (1969–71 = 100) 1977–79
Low-income countries	**187.1**	**15 718**	**239**	**0.9**	**2.8**	**10.2**	**25**	**46**	**91**
Low-income semiarid	**28.0**	**5745**	**187**	**0.0**	**3.3**	**10.0**	**17**	**43**	**88**
1. Chad	4.4	1284	110	−1.4	4.6	7.9	15*	41	91
2. Somalia	3.8	638	—	−0.5	4.5	11.3	60	44	85
3. Mali	6.8	1240	140	1.1	5.0	9.7	10	43	88
4. Upper Volta	5.6	274	180	0.3	1.3	9.8	5**	43	93
5. Gambia	0.6	11	250	2.6**	—	—	10**	42	77
6. Niger	5.2	1267	270	−1.3	2.1	10.8	8	43	89
7. Mauritania	1.6	1031	320	1.9	1.6	10.1	17*	43	75
Low-income other	**159.1**	**9973**	**247**	**1.0**	**2.8**	**10.7**	**27**	**47**	**91**
8. Ethiopia	30.9	1222	130	1.3	2.1	4.3	15*	40	84
9. Guinea-Bissau	0.8	36	170	—	—	—	7**	42	94
10. Burundi	4.0	28	180	2.1	2.8	11.2	25	42	105
11. Malawi	5.8	118	200	2.9	2.4	9.1	25*	47	100
12. Rwanda	4.9	26	200	1.5	13.1	14.6	—	47	107
13. Benin	3.4	113	250	0.6	1.9	9.2	7**	47	97
14. Mozambique	10.2	783	250	0.1	2.8	11.0	—	47	75
15. Sierra Leone	3.4	72	250	0.4	2.9	11.3	—	47	87
16. Tanzania	18.0	945	260	2.3	1.8	13.0	66*	52	94
17. Zaire	27.5	2345	260	0.7	29.9	31.4	15	47	90
18. Guinea	5.3	246	280	0.3	1.5	4.4	20*	44	86
19. Central African Rep.	2.0	623	290	0.7	4.1	9.1	—	44	102

21. Uganda	12.8	236	290	−0.2	3.0	28.3	—	54	90
22. Lesotho	1.3	30	340	6.0	2.5	11.6	52*	51	100
23. Togo	2.4	57	350	3.6	1.1	10.3	18	47	81
24. Sudan	17.9	2506	370	0.6	3.7	6.8	20*	47	105
Middle-income oil importers	**65.2**	**3690**	**532**	**1.5**	**2.4**	**9.9**	**34**	**50**	**95**
25. Kenya	15.3	583	380	2.7	1.5	11.1	45*	55	92
26. Ghana	11.3	239	400	−0.8	7.6	32.4	—	49	82
27. Senegal	5.5	197	430	−0.2	1.7	7.6	10*	43	88
28. Zimbabwe	7.1	391	470	0.8	1.3	8.4	—	55	100
29. Liberia	1.8	111	500	1.6	1.9	9.4	30	54	101
30. Zambia	5.6	753	500	0.8	7.6	6.8	39*	49	99
31. Cameroon	8.2	475	560	2.5	4.2	10.3	—	47	110
32. Swaziland	0.5	17	650	7.2**	—	—	65**	47	109
33. Botswana	0.8	600	720	9.1**	—	—	35**	49	89
34. Mauritius	0.9	2	1030	2.3**	—	—	80**	65	100
35. Ivory Coast	8.2	322	1040	2.4	2.8	13.5	20	47	102
Middle-income oil exporters	**91.6**	**2781**	**669**	**3.2**	**3.3**	**19.0**	**—**	**48**	**86**
36. Angola	6.9	1247	440	−2.1	3.3	21.6	—	42	85
37. Congo	1.5	342	630	0.9	5.4	10.9	—	42	85
38. Nigeria	82.6	924	670	3.7	2.6	19.0	—	49	87
39. Gabon	0.6	268	3280	6.1**	—	—	12**	45	94
Sub-Saharan Africa	**343.9**	**22 189**	**411**	**1.6**	**2.8**	**10.3**	**27**	**47**	**91**
All low-income countries	**2260.2**	**33 778**	**230**	**1.6**	**3.0**	**10.8**	**51**	**57**	**105**
All middle-income countries	**985.0**	**38 705**	**1420**	**3.8**	**3.0**	**13.3**	**72**	**61**	**107**
Industrialized countries	**671.2**	**30 430**	**9440**	**4.0**	**4.3**	**9.4**	**99**	**74**	**110**

Figures marked with an * are for years other than 1976.
SOURCE World Bank, *Agenda for Action*, 143.

economy. To be sure, this bourgeoisie retains important external and internal linkages, especially with foreign countries and corporations on the one hand and with domestic factions and forces on the other hand. Nevertheless, its ability to control the state and economy, in particular the direction of surplus distribution even if not the rate of surplus production, is growing as the 'independence generation' yields to a successor grouping of politicians, bureaucrats, soldiers and entrepreneurs. There is, of course, a debate about the basis and autonomy of this class as well as about the different fractions within it; this is treated in the next two chapters. Here, however, I note simply the existence of increasing differentiation within African states; the bourgeoisie has prospered and invested in its future while other classes have hardly increased their standards of living if at all. Indeed, in many African states the poor continue to get poorer: more marginal, more impoverished and more malnourished.

Second, inequalities *among* African political economies have also increased, particularly since the demise of the Bretton Woods system in the mid-1970s (contrast per capita GNPs between individual and groups of states in Table I·1). A few economies have benefited from the high price of oil – Algeria, Gabon, Libya and Nigeria – while many have been among the Most Seriously Affected, especially Ghana, Somalia, Tanzania and Upper Volta (see Table I·2). A few have weathered the storm better – e.g. Ivory Coast and Kenya – while others have had the process of decay intensified through unfavourable global conditions – e.g. Chad, Uganda and Zaire. In short, African political economies are more diverse and divergent now than at independence: a few Newly *Industrialising* Countries (NICs) – the 'semi-periphery' (see Chapter 1) – have been able to take advantage of the global shocks, whereas the majority of the 'real' periphery have suffered minimal or negative growth because of expensive energy, international inflation and recession, floating

TABLE 1·2 *Distribution of total African GDP, among subgroups of countries* (in percentage shares)

	1960	*1970*	*1980*
Major oil exporters	24.3	32.7	42.1
Non-oil exporters	74.6	65.8	56.3
Least developed countries	18.9	16.4	13.3
Developing Africa	100.0	100.0	100.0

SOURCE ECA secretariat and ECA *Silver Jubilee Anniversary Meetings*, April-May 1983 (E/ECA/CM.9/20).

exchange rates, and strict IMF conditions (compare pre- and post-1970 growth rates in Table I·3).[13]

TABLE I·3 *Growth of GNP per person in Africa, 1960–90*

Country groups	*GNP per person (1980 current dollars)*	*Annual growth of GNP* 1960–70	1970–80	Low case 1980–90	High case 1980–90
Sub-Saharan Africa					
Low-income oil importers	260	1.7	−0.4	−1.0	0.1
Middle-income oil importers	520	1.7	0.4	0.0	0.3
Oil exporters	730	0.4	2.6	2.0	2.3
All developing countries	850	3.5	2.7	2.2	3.3
Low-income	250	1.8	1.6	1.5	2.6
Middle-income	1580	3.9	2.8	2.2	3.4

SOURCES World Bank, *Agenda for Action*, 122 and *World Development Report 1981*, table 1.1.

These inequalities within and among African states are, of course, interrelated. There have always been close links between indigenous rulers and foreign interests, whether in trade, technology or tactic;[14] these have survived, albeit in revised form, the colonial interregnum when, except under so-called 'indirect rule' regimes, local rulers were subordinated to foreign overlords. Now the tables have been turned once more and African interests can expel and exclude external interests should they wish to do so. In practice they rarely exercise this option, preferring to modify the 'balance of power' over time through almost continuous negotiation: Africa remains a vulnerable as well as open continent.

The 'transnational' interaction between African and non-African, historically European but now also American and Japanese, bourgeoisies – one strand in the 'world ruling class'[15] – is one way in which external changes have come to affect internal development, especially in certain distinctive states as noted below. Whether by invitation (semi-industrialisation), by coincidence (energy or mineral resources), or by 'conspiracy' (strategic location or leadership), a few African leaders have been able to augment their influence and income by securing specially favourable arrangements with foreign countries, corporations and classes.

By contrast to the upward mobility of a few African bourgeoisies and political economies, the majority in the periphery endure minimal or negative opportunities. Internal inequalities tend to be larger inside the semi-periphery than in the periphery although the rate of growth, but not of development, is higher. This uneven incidence of growth has led to a renewed interest in 'self-reliance' as a strategy to maximise development, particularly in situations of an unsatisfactory experience of expansion as endured by a growing group of countries and classes in the contemporary period.

PRESSURES FOR AND PROSPECTS OF SELF-RELIANCE

Self-reliance, the new motto of the continent, can be conceived in two different ways: as strategy or as inevitability, and in national or in collective guises. As strategy it has been espoused in both African and Third World forums particularly in the seventies in both national and collective forms. Non-Aligned State Conferences since Lusaka in 1970 have, in general, been increasingly preoccupied by the elusiveness of development: self-reliance has been advocated as being both compatible with, and an assurance against the non-appearance of, any New International Economic Order (NIEO).[16] And, in particular, the 1980 Lagos economic summit marked the adoption of self-reliance at national, regional and continental levels in Africa. As strategy, then, self-reliance is a reaction to the existential and intellectual deficiencies of 'developmentalism':

> The growing acceptance of national and collective self-reliance as a development strategy represents a victory for scholars who, during the 1960s and 1970s, have championed what is termed 'dependency' theory.
>
> [The] call for national and collective Third World self-reliance efforts [is] to bring about indigenous or self-sustaining development. Unlike the 1960s development strategy, which emphasised Third World integration into the global economy, the new strategy's hallmark is a giant step back from full participation in the international economy. Selective and limited participation in the global economy is emphasised until such time that economic relationships between nations become more symmetrical.[17]

The economic potential of and class constellation behind self-reliance as strategy is examined in Part II. Here I merely note the possibility of such a policy as inevitability rather than as choice. Given the current neo-mercantilist predisposition of major Western governments, established transnational class and product exchanges are no longer so popular or profitable. Rather, the advanced industrialised states are increasingly disinterested in the periphery, although their interest in the semi-periphery may increase almost in proportion to its decline in the former, Fourth World. Therefore, to avoid the humiliation of differentiation or *triage* as practised by leading First World regimes, several enlightened leaders in the periphery have moved towards self-reliance. That is, they have attempted to turn the contemporary crisis in the world system into a conjuncture; to take advantage of it by coming to rely on indigenous resources, technologies and processes, seeking to satisfy domestic Basic Human Needs (BHN) before external demands.

CHARACTER OF, AND CONTRADICTIONS IN, THE AFRICAN CRISIS

Self-reliance at the level of ideology and economic decline at the level of production are symptomatic of the African crisis. This possible conjuncture is marked by a distinctive constellation of international and internal forces: protectionism and differentiation globally and decay and contradiction domestically. The previous major conjuncture of this type was the depression of the 1930s – the breeding ground of African nationalism – so the recession of the 1970s may come to be seen as equally important. As Basil Davidson suggests, 'Up to 1939, the important point of change since 1890 was not the First World War. It was the great slump which began in Europe and America in 1929 and hit the colonies of Africa a year or so later.'[18] Such a focus on substructure rather than superstructure remains important for the present and future of African political economies; this level of analysis is adopted throughout the volume. And post-expansion tensions are not confined to the Third or Fourth Worlds.

Rather, the recession and the response of monetarism have served to intensify latent antagonisms in the centre too: more national versus more international fractions – a major divide being between those which are in the state capitalist versus those in multinational corporate sectors – are one feature of 'inter-imperial rivalries' among the advanced industrialised states. Such inter- and intra-country and corporate tensions are focused in particular on the semi-periphery, one of the few areas of relative expansion in a contracting world economy. But competition there may, by contrast, intensify the relative neglect of the real periphery.

The inclination to isolation apparent among certain metropolitan countries and corporations in terms of economic preferences may be in opposition to the continued interventive tendencies apparent among decision-makers in strategic sectors. Notwithstanding the inherent instability of the semi-periphery (see Chapter 4), great powers may still attempt to retreat somewhat from their global economic and strategic reach by attempting to build up relatively strong regional centres: 'sub-imperial' powers.[19] The appearance and resilience of such centres within the periphery is a function not only of the emergence of a national bourgeoisie in such states but also of metropolitan insistence and peripheral powerlessness, assuming general global economic conditions do not deteriorate further. As Philippe Lemaitre indicates, local–multinational linkages assure

> a flow of technology, military equipment, and advanced machinery into the state in exchange for certain key products. The corporations and the major extra-African countries in which they were based would gain assured markets, profits from the sale of invisibles, and the flow of needed raw materials. In return, the middle classes of semi-industrialising countries would be in a position to obtain advanced equipment, enhance the military security of the state, and carve out a local sector of the world market for intermediate industry.[20]

Whilst such poles of relative affluence may serve to salvage some faith in orthodox development theory, their position and prosperity are a function of continued uneven expansion of the world economy rather than indications of inward-looking autonomous development. Furthermore, as such regional centres begin to acquire a degree of industrialisation and sophistication they may come to demand improved conditions for their co-operation: their expansion may come to be seen as a cause of 'deindustrialisation' in the metropole, giving rise to tensions between economic and strategic interests in the latter. Moreover, regional resentment and opposition in the African periphery may increase the cost of such collaboration for both metropole and semi-periphery. As I. William Zartman indicates, relating regional inequalities to global conditions:

> By the 1980s, the spread in the level of power sources is certain to increase, even dramatically. Within the decade, Algeria or Nigeria may be more developed economically than South Africa . . . Several effects are likely to ensue. First, the more developed members may become more attractive to outside influence, even if greater amounts of influence will now be required in order to have an effect. Second . . . internal gaps between socio-economic levels are likely to be magnified, as are also gaps between the states which surged forward and those many others which have been unable to do so . . . the chances for regional leadership are increased.[21]

Such inequalities are central to this analysis, and their material bases as well as apparent characteristics are probed; i.e. the structure of Newly *Influential* Countries cannot be divorced from their situation as Newly Industrialising Countries. Likewise, the political economy of the periphery is a fundamental feature of its marginality. In short, the substructure of Africa and its incorporation into the world system is the primary determinant of its development prospect and diplomatic position. In other words, the present and future of the continent cannot be understood without looking at a set of major contradictions, antagonistic or not, within and between the states of Africa. The continental dialectic is central to both prognosis and projection: neither analysis nor prescription can be taken out of the context of particular political economies, national, regional and global.

Given the range of such political economies in Africa, no single set of social relations is likely to be found in all of them; a neo-Marxist approach takes it for granted that modes and relations of production are diverse. However, whilst some states are more capitalist than others none are advanced industrialised societies. Therefore the dominant dialectic of industrialised states in formation – that between the bourgeoisie and proletariat – is neither present nor salient in Africa. Rather, depending on the presence or not of non-capitalist modes and of mining or manufacturing, the continent's political economies include a rich range of classes and coalitions. In particular, this analysis will concentrate on several emergent fractions and antagonisms (see Chapter 2): national versus transnational elements within the indigenous bourgeoisie, proletariat (including any labour aristocracy) versus peasantry, various fractions within the petty-bourgeoisie, and the position and potential of the underemployed and unemployed. The role of some of these classes will be more pronounced in some (e.g. national bourgeoisie in the semi-periphery) than in other political economies, while in some states single fractions may be hegemonic (e.g. indigenous petty-bourgeoisie in post-Tolbert Liberia) whereas in others complex, 'corporatist' coalitions may be the basis of power (e.g. transnational bourgeoisie – traditional aristocracy alliance in Shagari's Nigeria contrasted with an indigenous proletarian–peasant alliance in Machel's Mozambique).[22]

The character of the 'domestic' social structure in such dependent states is closely related to 'external' inequalities, both having increased and intensified in recent years. It is almost a tautology, but clearly the bourgeoisie is central to the development of NICs on the continent; similarly, the peasantry is vital to continued growth in commodity-exporting parts of the periphery while the proletariat remains powerful in mineral-producing territories. In none do the conditions for socialism through struggle seem conducive; hence the frequency of socialism by declaration, as a substitute for mobilisation and organisation. Only in those few settler colonies where black rule has been resisted and delayed have social conditions and consciousness produced truly radical nationalist movements; hence the relatively promising prospects for a sustained transition to socialism in Angola, Mozambique and Zimbabwe (and, in the future, South Africa?).

These divergencies both within and between states are factors in Africa's increasingly disparate foreign policies: their social bases generate distinctive sets of linkages with the world system.[23] Hence the propensity towards disunity in the OAU as sadly displayed at the 1982 Tripoli non-summits: the issue is not so much Angola, Chad or the Sahara but the centrifugal pressures of different political economies. Contemporary forces are unlikely to converge for the foreseeable future. Rather, all indications point to more and not less inequality on the continent. So disunity is unlikely to be a transitory phenomenon; instead, divergencies are likely to intensify.

FROM CRISIS TO CONJUNCTURE?

The projection of inequalities in the future has profound implications for both policy and politics; hence the 'great debate' as the 1980s open about the continent's development strategy.[24] The alternative World Bank and OAU plans for Africa are based on different assumptions, expectations and projections; they also reflect distinctive class preferences. *Agenda for Action* favours bourgeois and NIC interests whereas the *Lagos Plan of Action* is based on more proletarian and peasant BHN characteristics of the periphery. If *Agenda* became the continental plan then further inter- and intra-state inequalities would ensue. If, however, the *Lagos Plan of Action* was adopted such inequalities might be contained or even reduced. In short, these two plans reflect different class and country interests both at present and in prospect, as examined further in Chapter 3.

The current and projected condition of the continent is depressing, notwithstanding the utility and vitality of the debate about alternative development strategies:[25] intra- and inter-state inequalities are likely to continue their ineluctable increases with profound implications for national and continental order and development. Adedeji articulates the atmosphere of depression well:

> The reality of today is that after two decades of political independence for most African countries, the economic emancipation that was expected to follow closely on the heels of political independence still remains only a hope. . . . Thus, the African economy today is the most open and the most exposed economy in the world, overly dependent on external trade and other external stimuli, foreign technology, and foreign expertise. The very strategies of development the African governments have been procuring since independence have come from theories of economic development that were developed during the colonial and neocolonial periods to rationalise the colonial pattern of production in Africa . . . neither high rates of growth or diversification nor an increasing measure of self-reliance and self-sustainment has been achieved in the African economy.[26]

Given such an unsatisfactory inheritance and trend, Adedeji calls for a more authentic strategy based on indigenous needs, values and lifestyles. He suggests, idealistically, that the 'very dismal forecasts' can only be avoided if an African-oriented programme contains 'certain basic elements':

> These are self-reliance and self-sustaining development, democratisation of the development process, dealienation, the creation of the right political and social environments, the recovery of

> self-confidence by the peoples of Africa, and the willingness to achieve effective and meaningful cooperation among African states.[27]

Adedeji also asserts that the time has come to progress beyond declaration towards implementation. For just as socialism cannot survive if based only on resolutions so self-reliance will be vulnerable if based only on documents. The socialism being forged in, say, Angola, Ethiopia and Mozambique is, therefore, more resilient than that in Benin, Somalia or Tanzania precisely because it is based on struggle among particular social forces rather than on the declarations of party congresses or presidents.

Likewise, the realisation of self-reliance at national, regional or continental levels may be more and not less likely because of the gloomy projections and gathering contradictions, as indicated in the conclusion. The processes of class formation and relation have accelerated and intensified since independence, especially since the mid-1970s. The deepening dialectic attendant on the current conjuncture may bring foward forces and frameworks to resolve Africa's condition and crisis. The superstructural debates about alternative development strategies may merely reflect, then, the evolution of substructure as established plans and policies reveal their own deficiencies. In short, the crisis has begun to throw up its own contradictions, out of which new coalitions and strategies may emerge. The contemporary situation will not be totally negative, then, if it generates the conditions under which social pressures can be developed, sustained, and resolved: a 'willed future' as advocated in current ECA terminology.[28] Given the rapidity with which the African crisis is gathering, unpromising projections may yet be transcended because the assumptions on which they were based have been transformed: a conjuncture, not just a crisis.[29]

Yet the African revolution is quite unlikely to be either comprehensive or conclusive given the variety of internal and international interests and institutions involved. Once begun, however, it may prove to be unstoppable; hence the reservations of some current leaders about self-reliance. The projection of pessimistic trends and the suggestion of alternative strategies is thus just one aspect of the contemporary crisis, one that adds to the dialectic and encourages resolution through revolution, i.e. a conjuncture.

As indicated in the chapters which follow, the dynamic of change in Africa has two particular cores, one structural the other spatial. First, the structural force is the increasing impoverishment and marginalisation of non-bourgeois classes almost everywhere on the continent as inflation, recession and decline undermine the legacy and logic of dependent growth. And second, the spatial factor is the intensifying conflict in southern Africa, both within the already 'liberated' territories and around the remaining racist regimes of Namibia and South Africa: the escalation and expansion of 'destabilisation'. The characters of the political economies of Angola, Mozambique and Zimbabwe and of the struggles for Namibia and South Africa will affect social situations and conflicts throughout the continent.

If proletarian and peasant interests emerge victorious in both independent and southern Africa then the character of Africa's political economy and projected future may be transformed. If, however, enough growth and repression enable bourgeois dominance to be sustained in independent Africa and 'neo-colonial' solutions are realised in southern Africa then the African revolution may be postponed until the next century.

Most likely, of course, is a scenario involving elements from both these polar futures: some radical regimes in independent and Southern Africa but also some authoritarian and expansive governments as well. As Steven Langdon and Lynn Mytelka assert in their own preview of the continent, progressive elements in both situations are interrelated although the outcome of the dialectic is not assured in terms of either result or time-scale:

> Armed conflict in southern Africa . . . is likely to be no more than the most dramatic African form of confrontation between dependence and self-reliance in the 1980s. We expect the contradictions of periphery capitalism in Africa to become more acute in most countries on the continent in the next decade, and we expect the struggles for change in such countries to become more bitter as a result. We are confident, however, that out of such conflict can come more equitable and self-reliant development strategies that benefit the great majority of Africans.[30]

This book is concerned with this transition, in its intellectual as well as developmental forms.[31] That the continent has arrived at a critical conjuncture is incontrovertible. Yet the outcome of this contemporary dialectic – a crisis with or without resolution – is problematic. Hopefully, the following analysis will clarify some of the central issues and forces even if it cannot predict the character of the eventual synthesis: the coalitions of classes which will control Africa's political economies into the twenty-first century.

As John Saul has argued, such nuanced neo-Marxism may enable us to avoid the Scylla of modernisation theory and the Charybdis of Marxist dogma: a subtle perspective is needed to comprehend the African condition:

> to avoid excessive reliance not only upon the bluff, common-sensical insights into day-to-day events but also upon the procrustean, depoliticising determinism – often illuminating almost in spite of itself – of various recent 'Marxist' innovations in the field of radical Africana. Certainly some kind of analytical way forward is necessary if we are to forge an approach to politics adequate to the tasks which face the African revolution.[32]

The imperative of such analytic progress is reinforced by Immanuel Wallerstein's lament for conservative scholarship on Africa. This is especially so in the light of the current economic contraction which increases the prospects of regression and anarchy in practice as well as in theory:

> The years 1945–70 were a period of exceptional obscurantism in all fields of study, and African studies has been in this sense typical . . . If the decline of Cold War polarisation in the 1960s effectively reduced the political bargaining power of African states, the beginning of the worldwide economic contraction of effective demand of the 1970s is likely to sweep African aspirations aside as those who are on top of the world heap struggle with each other to remain there. In the 1960s, African scholars began to worry about 'growth without development'. In the 1970s and 1980s, there is the clear possibility of neither growth nor development.[33]

The following chapters examine Africa's current crisis given the continuing elusiveness of both growth and development. Even if the level of economic growth remains unsatisfactory, maybe the level of analytic development can be raised. And out of improved analysis may come appropriate *praxis:* the enhanced and sustained satisfaction of the Basic Human Needs of Africa's peoples. But before going forward, the first chapter goes backwards: to the unsatisfactory economic and theoretical inheritance of the continent at independence.

Part I

The African Crisis

1 Problematique: The State of the State

> 'The most general characteristic of [a modern political system] is the relatively high degree of differentiation, explicitness, and functional distinctiveness of political and governmental structures.'—James C. Coleman, 'Conclusion: the political systems of the developing areas', in Gabriel A. Almond and James C. Coleman (eds), *The Politics of Developing Areas* (Princeton: Princeton University Press, 1960) p. 532.

> '[Just] as the economic system of the periphery cannot be understood by itself, because its relations with the centre are crucial, so the social structure of the periphery is a mutilated structure, which cannot be understood unless it is properly situated: as an element in a *world* social structure.'—Samir Amin, *Accumulation on a World Scale* (New York: Monthly Review, 1974) Second Volume, 360.

> 'Class analysis of contemporary Africa has had a shaky history.'—Immanuel Wallerstein, 'Class and Class Conflict in Africa', *Monthly Review,* 26(9), February 1975, p. 34.

Independence in Africa served to increase significantly the number and range of state structures, much to the delight of political and other social scientists who so often substitute typology for theory. The first decade of independence was marked, then, by the presentation of alternative frameworks by which to categorise the polities of Africa. The second decade consisted of an attempt to substitute alternative categories while the current, third decade is marked by a determination to abandon such inappropriate approaches and to substitute a more critical and materialist typology. At best, established frameworks are considered to be misleading and moribund; at worst, they are treated as adjuncts of dominant capitalist formations. Foster-Carter has articulated the latter view:

> A basic aspect of neo-Marxist development theory has been its critique of its bourgeois rivals and their application to specific problems. Bourgeois development theory, which purports to be value-free science, is exposed as ideology, deliberately or otherwise serving Western foreign policy and economic interests or reflecting Western prejudices.[1]

The first independence decade was marked by two mammoth exercises in such an establishment mould, opening in 1960 with the Almond and Coleman collection on *The Politics of Developing Areas* and closing in 1970 with the Coleman and Rosberg companion volume on *Political Parties and National Integration in Tropical Africa.* By contrast, Samir Amin's major works appeared in the mid-1970s, at least in English, to be joined in the early 1980s by second generation critiques such as *A Political Economy of Africa* from Claude Ake.[2]

FROM POLITICAL MODERNISATION TO POLITICAL ECONOMY

The classic work on Africa in the 'political modernisation' genre by James Coleman is characterised by a static and superstructural framework. The focus is on national integration; political co-operation is largely assumed. In general, it is taken to be axiomatic that the higher the level of attributes of 'modernity' such as urbanisation, commercialisation and secularisation the greater the degree of 'national integration' through political functions such as socialisation, aggregation and communication. So in his essay on 'The Politics of sub-Saharan Africa', Coleman proposes a fourfold framework: no party, one party dominant, comprehensive nationalist and competitive party systems.[3] He expands this typology in his conclusion to the whole collection – 'The political systems of the developing areas' – by recognising authoritarian as well as semi-competitive and competitive systems given the slow march towards modernity.[4] Coleman subdivides his 'oligarchy' category into three – colonial/racial, conservative, and traditional – and his 'democracy' type into four – political, tutelary, terminal colonial, and modernising.[5] This penchant for categorising is continued in his second major opus of that initial decade – *Political Parties and National Integration in Tropical Africa* – co-edited with Carl Rosberg. To salvage the expectation of increasing pluralism given gradual modernisation, concepts such as 'functional load' and 'political consolidation' are introduced to produce another fourfold typology for Africa: 'pragmatic–pluralistic', 'revolutionary–centralising', 'transforming historic oligarchies', and 'expanding political scale'.[6] And at the start of the new decade, in response to both the new orthodoxy of political economy and the new intolerance of incumbent leaders, Rosberg in co-operation with Robert Jackson produced a long-awaited sequel to and revision of the modernisation mode.[7] With a focus on the individual rather than the party in power, Jackson and Rosberg offer a personalistic rejoinder to the structuralists of both functionalist and materialist persuasion. In a reminiscent typology, they identify princes, autocrats, prophets and tyrants as the determinants of power in Africa: the surrogates of institutions.[8] And they justify their non-Marxist perspective, with its almost exclusive focus on superstructure, particularly the individual and political, thus:

> [The] existence of personal systems is dependent less upon the underlying socio-economic environment . . . The ruler has the greatest influence in determining . . . issues in African personal regimes . . . how well he performs . . . [is] crucial to the stability of the polity and the persistence of the regime.
>
> The two most clearly discernible dimensions of state-building during the last two decades of African independence have been the bureaucratisation of the instruments of state power and the legalisation of the discretionary powers of personal rulers: a trend towards state organisation rather than institutionalisation . . . Personal rule can be expected to continue as a central characteristic of African states, probably with a trend towards greater organisational and legal authoritarianism.[9]

Such typologies, old and new, do not capture very much of the reality of contemporary African political economies – how to explain decline as well as aggrandisement? – primarily because they deal almost exclusively with superstructure rather than substructure; they do not incorporate any concern for modes and relations of production. Instead, they focus on the characteristics of regimes and parties in isolation from their social base. Vernon McKay summed up the deficient state of the field in the mid-1960s:

> Among numerous attempts to classify African states in recent years, the most common system divides them into radical, moderate, and conservative camps.[10]

This type of superficial, simplistic approach was increasingly recognised to be inadequate as the limits of independence were revealed. Common acceptance of the modernisation 'paradigm' was relatively shortlived, therefore, as Wallerstein indicates:

> [By] 1960, scholars seemed to converge in an effort to bury class analysis in Africa. However, the 1960s were a traumatic decade for Africa in many ways.[11]

Hence the apparent readiness by the end of the first independence decade to begin to look at other approaches to African politics-cum-economics. Given the inadequacies of such modernisation formulations for either policy or *praxis,* given changes in the global system with all their implications for Africa and other parts of the Third World, Samir Amin has argued that a world view is an imperative:

> [Just] as the economic system of the periphery cannot be understood by itself, because its relations with the centre are crucial, so the social structure of the periphery is a multilated structure, which cannot be understood unless it is properly situated: as an element in a *world* social structure.[12]

Amin has offered such a global and historical analysis himself by (i) identifying changes in the pattern of African incorporation over time and (ii) proposing a typology of various forms of incorporation. First, he identifies three precolonial *phases* – premercantilist, mercantilist and integration into the full capitalist system – and, second, he proposes three *types* of incorporation – Africa of the labour reserves (Southern and Eastern), Africa of the colonial trade economy (West) and Africa of the concession-owning companies (Central).[13] These two sets of distinctions are based on patterns of production and exchange rather than on the character – racial, ethnic or politica – of the coloniser or colonised.

In addition to the imperatives of historical and global perspectives, Amin insists on a materialist approach, one which contrasts not only development between centre and periphery, but also that within different parts of the periphery:

> The African pattern of development of capitalism is thus different from the Eastern and Latin American patterns as regards the fundamental point of the respective places occupied by the rural and urban bourgeoisies and the relations between these two classes.[14]

This central question of the character of the bourgeoisie in Africa is examined further below, and an alternative analytic framework is proposed in the next chapter. Here I just pause to note that the distinctive development of capitalism on the continent has implications for politics. Not that we should revert to the 'primordial' concerns of Coleman *et al.* with oligarchic and other party systems; simply that we should recognise the continuing interplay between class-type and other social forces. Ethnicity, religion and region – the bases of 'fractional' or 'sectional' support – cannot be excluded just because they do not fit easily into an orthodox Marxist framework.[15] Instead, our 'neo-Marxism' must be able to incorporate such salient relations, as indeed it now must in advanced industrialised countries too. Moreover, as Ian Roxborough suggests, it must recognise the powerful role of external as well as internal class elements:

> The class structures of the Third World differ from those of the advanced nations in two principal ways: they are more complex, and the classes themselves are usually much weaker . . . Not only are the class structures of the under-developed nations complex and weak, they are also 'incomplete' in the sense that the dominant class, or one fraction of the dominant class is absent. This is the case where the dominant class or fraction thereof is foreign.[16]

Amin reinforces these points in two separate ways. First, he recognises the continued salience of non-class links, even in ostensibly class-type relations:

> [The] development of capitalism in Black Africa remains embryonic, in the sense that vestiges of the past, especially the survival of structures that are still living realities (tribal ties, for example), often continue to hide the new structures (ties based on class, or on groups defined by their position in the capitalist system).[17]

And second, given the continued place of foreign fractions in the bourgeoisie, as well as the delayed development of an urban and industrial indigenous bourgeoisie, the national political economy has a distinctive character:

> The new bureaucracy tends in these circumstances to become the principal driving force in society. The relations between this social group on the one hand, and, on the other, the bourgeoisies arisen from the planters and from small-scale urban business, and foreign capital, constitute the essence of the problem of relations between political power and economic responsibility in these countries.[18]

THE EMERGENCE OF AN AFRICAN BOURGEOISIE

The underdevelopment and extroversion of the national bourgeoisie in Africa have major implications for the character of class relations on the continent. However, although this indigenous bourgeoisie developed slowly because of the dominance of imposed colonial rulers and established rural leaders, it has begun to exert its hegemony as foreign and traditional fractions yield to indigenous urban elements, both bureaucratic and entrepreneurial as well as military. Not that these are entirely autonomous from either internal (traditional and ethnic) or external (corporate and governmental) linkages. As Shivji asserts in his rejection of any dogmatic structural Marxism which denies the importance of independence:

> In a neo-colonial state, state power rests in the hands of a local class or classes which constitute the ruling class. This class or classes have their own class interests arising from the place they occupy in social production, which in the longer run coincide with the interests of imperialism as a whole.[19]

This coincidence of interest in the contemporary period is particularly ironic given the historic differences between metropolitan and peripheral capitalisms. Indeed, it is these differences which explain the weakness of indigenous bourgeois elements in the first years of independence. However, through the judicious use of state power the latter have begun to reverse this inherited inferiority. They have been aided in this by current contradictions apparent within the advanced industrialised states in which protectionist governments and expansionist companies have divergent attitudes towards recession and inflation.

The global reach of the multinational corporation is thus being restricted in the present decade by contrast to the previous twenty years, not so much because of nationalist tendencies in the Third World as because of mercantilist inclinations in the First. Moreover, the bourgeoisie in the First World is no longer so protestant and diligent in its drive for surplus accumulation and social reproduction. So Foster-Carter's scepticism about the inheritance and position of the new bourgeoisies is rather misplaced, at least for the present, post-industrialised order:

> They are incapable (as Fanon has insisted) of carrying out the classic progressive role of the European bourgeoisie. Herein lies a vicious paradox: the incapacity of *indigenous* capitalism is rooted in the effects of *foreign* capitalism's [imperialism's] concomitant inability to promote development.[20]

Although some bourgeoisies in Africa may still lack the capacity to develop themselves, many bureaucratic, entrepreneurial and military fractions have acquired such an ability. This is especially so in those states at the semi-periphery which have been able to grow at a faster rate than those at the periphery. Moreover, those with particular strategic resources or positions have been able to extract more favourable conditions in negotiations with First World countries and corporations than the more marginal countries. As Shivji suggests:

> The various neo-colonial ruling classes exhibit different degrees of independence from particular imperialist powers, in line with the conjuncture of class alliances and struggle at particular times.[21]

FROM 'NEW STATES' TO 'PERIPHERAL SOCIAL FORMATIONS'

Taken together, then, these historic and current conditions constitute the broad parameters within which peripheral social formations in Africa have been formed. First, the colonial dominance, now declining, of foreign capital; second, the continuing importance of traditional and rural bourgeoisies; and third, the difficulties, external and internal, confronting the emergence of bureaucratic, entrepreneurial and military fractions. Amin has succinctly summarised the basic characteristics of such formations:

> All the peripheral formations thus share three essential features: i) the predominance of agrarian and commercial capitalism in the national sector of the economy; ii) the creation of a local bourgeoisie in the wake of dominant foreign capital; iii) the tendency to a peculiar bureaucratic form of development which is characteristic of the periphery in our own day.[22]

But neither centre–periphery nor class relations in the periphery are static; contradictions at both and between both levels generate change as indicated in Chapter 3. Hence the need to go beyond the dependent 'new state' perspective even in the periphery, what James Petras has called the 'collaborator state':

> First, it is a penetrated society . . . the class structure is penetrated by imperial interests. State and societal *penetration* is matched by the organisation and direction of the economy toward a *complementary role* within the imperial division of labour. Thus the *kind* of goods produced, the terms of exchange all maximise gains to the imperial centre and the principal classes and institutional members within the collaborator state.[23]

The problematical nature of social change in such an open peripheral state – one in which dependence is the primary force – is restated by Robert Brenner, who nonetheless recognises the possibility of such a transition under certain conditions:

> True bourgeois revolutions are not on the agenda [in the Third World]; international capitalists, local capitalists and neo-fascists alike have remained, by and large, interested in and supportive of the class structure of underdevelopment . . . Until recently, of course, the class interests behind 'industrialisation via import substitution' have not, as a rule, been strong enough to force the class structural shifts that would open the way to profitable investment in development.[24]

Now, however, such a shift may indeed by possible, because of changes in both centre–periphery relations and relations within the periphery itself. First, with the demise of the post-war Bretton Woods order, economic recession and contraction in the North have generated inter-imperial rivalries which have important implications for fractions in the South. As Shivji indicates:

> In a neo-colonial situation, the inter-imperialist rivalries come to have a full weight because the various factions and classes in the local state power forge alliances with different imperialist powers in line with their own interests. Both the internal class contradictions and the inter-imperial rivalries are reflected in the constant political turbulence and reorganisation of the ruling blocs in these countries. Thus, power in the neo-colonial state is imbued with the crisis of hegemony, popularly interpreted as political instability.[25]

And second, class accumulation and reproduction in the South have begun to produce a more self-conscious and self-confident *national* bourgeoisie, particularly within the semi-periphery, with its more propitious circumstances. As Petras points out:

> The conditions under which accumulation takes place include: a) the nature of the state (and state policy); and b) class relations (process of surplus extraction, intensity of exploitation, level of class struggle, concentration of the work force).[26]

Hence the need to look at national as well as international contradictions.

The emergence of distinct and dialectical fractions within the African bourgeoisie is inseparable from changes in both local and global political economies. In the former, the hegemony of established traditional, political, comprador, and bureaucratic has given way under pressure to the emergence of national, technocratic and military fractions. Meanwhile in the latter, inter-imperial rivalries and the deindustrialisation of established economies have led to the decline of some countries, sectors, companies and classes. In Britain, steel, British Leyland and workers are examples of a transformation in modes and relations of production in the North, while the intrusion of military regimes, technological imperatives and indigenous capital are in the South. Together such transitions have come to redefine the neo-colonial nexus in the present post-OPEC era.

CONTRADICTIONS AT THE SEMI-PERIPHERY

I turn to a general typology of social forces on the continent as well as to particular combinations thereof in the following chapter. Here I simply note the centrality of the semi-periphery in the prospects for capitalist development in Africa. For it is in this minority of political economies that social contradictions and state policies are relatively advanced; it is here that the national bourgeoisie will grow, if at all. As Petras suggests, based on his own enquiry into change in Latin America and elsewhere:

> The analysis points to the centrality of the advanced regions of the Third World as the epicentres of social revolution. From this perspective, social revolution is not a product of a *passing* movement of modernisation but an *approaching* phase: heightened class conflict accompanies capital maturity.[27]

It is in just such semi-peripheral states that social contradictions between national and transnational bourgeoisies, between 'modern' and 'traditional' fractions, and between capital and labour are most intense precisely because of the rapidity and intensity of economic growth and social change. As Petras notes himself:

> Three major subimperialist powers – Iran, Brazil and South Africa – are experiencing major political crises that could eventually lead to fundamental societal and economic changes. Shifts in power, regime and social system have already, or may, occur[ed] within these and other countries, whose economies are, or have been, among the fastest growing in the Third World.[28]

Wallerstein has put such contradictions at the semi-periphery in historical and global perspective, the resolution of which would have, as we will see particularly in the cases of Nigeria and South Africa, profound implications for the direction of development in the rest of the continent:

> The semi-peripheral states in the coming decades will be a battleground of two major transnational forces. One will be the multinational corporations who will be fighting for the survival of the essentials of the capitalist system: the probability of continued surplus appropriation on a world scale. The other will be a transnational alignment of socialist forces who will be seeking to undermine the capitalist world economy, not by 'developing' singly, but by forcing relatively drastic redistributions of world surplus and cutting the long-term present and potential organisational links between multinationals and certain strata internal to

> each semi-peripheral country, including such strata in the socialist semi-peripheral states.[29]

I look at the character of contemporary class coalitions in the semi-periphery in the next chapter, merely noting here the centrality of this minority of states in the overall continental order. Of course, such a conjuncture – intensified class conflict because of rapid economic growth – is probable in just a minority of African states, those which retain close 'transnational' class linkages, as well as contain the seeds of a national bourgeoisie. Hence the struggle within them as Wallerstein indicates in the previous citation. But the real periphery of the Fourth World also contains elements of such debates, even if its claims to growth and attention are increasingly minimal.

THE MARGINALISATION OF THE PERIPHERY

The majority in the Fourth, as opposed to the Third, World no longer enjoy – if that is the right emotive term – such links. Instead, given protectionist pressures in a post-industrial North, they are increasingly marginalised in terms of both exchange (see Table 1·1) and structure: the external element of the effective bourgeoisie – the corporate manager – is no longer overly concerned about their fate, unlike more paternalist governors of yesteryear. To be sure, some interests within certain advanced industrialised states may retain vestigial relations; and at times of economic or strategic crises these may be revived for a short while. But the overall trend in the 'post-colonial' world is towards a new distance between First and Fourth Worlds, the latter being concentrated in Africa. As Krishan Kumar warns in his review of the future of such non-industrialised states:

> The less-developed world, although it could well be ignored by the more developed, cannot but be affected by it. Just as in the earlier process of industrialisation the progress of some societies acted to constrain, retard, or distort the development of others, so as the rich societies move into a newer phase of their evolution [post-industrialism] will they continue to have an impact on the rest of the world, although their sins may now be those of omission rather than of commission.[30]

TABLE 1·1 *Africa's share of world and developing country exports of selected commodities*

Commodity	*Exports of selected primary commodities of Sub-Saharan countries as a percentage*					
	Of exports of those products of all the developing countries			*Of exports of those products of the whole world*		
	1960	*1970–2*	*1976–8*	*1960*	*1970–2*	*1976–8*
Fuels						
Petroleum	0.3	7.6	8.6	0.3	5.5	7.7
Minerals and metals						
Copper	47.3	52.1	38.8	25.5	28.2	19.2
Iron ore	10.8	30.3	19.7	4.3	11.4	8.1
Bauxite	5.7	4.7	31.7	4.8	3.4	27.7
Phosphate rock	0.6	13.3	14.3	0.4	7.1	9.4
Manganese ore	22.2	53.1	36.9	15.5	29.8	14.1
Zinc	27.7	25.9	18.7	6.8	5.7	3.6
Tin	11.7	9.7	3.6	10.7	8.3	3.0
Lead	12.9	19.4	6.6	4.8	4.1	2.2
Food and beverages						
Coffee	19.3	29.3	29.1	18.8	28.3	26.8
Cocoa	72.8	80.1	72.3	72.8	80.1	69.3
Sugar	4.6	5.6	11.0	3.4	4.0	4.5
Tea	7.1	15.7	19.4	6.2	13.1	15.7
Groundnuts	87.1	74.8	63.5	76.8	53.5	35.5
Groundnut oil	77.3	72.2	56.8	57.0	55.7	43.2
Beef	4.5	4.0	8.6	1.3	1.2	1.6
Palmoil	65.7	22.6	6.7	63.2	20.8	5.7
Bananas	11.3	7.2	4.9	10.6	6.6	4.6
Maize	4.8	4.4	2.5	1.6	1.0	0.4
Nonfood						
Timber	44.7	22.8	18.5	36.1	5.7	5.1
Cotton	23.2	28.8	22.4	10.3	16.3	11.3
Tobacco	40.6	25.4	19.4	11.2	6.7	8.9
Rubber	7.4	7.9	4.9	5.9	7.7	4.8
Hides and skins	21.2	33.7	23.7	7.9	7.9	4.4
Sisal	68.5	58.3	52.8	62.9	56.8	51.8

SOURCE World Bank, *Agenda for Action*, 21 and *Commodity Trade and Price Trends*.

However, as noted in the introduction there may be something of a contradiction in extra-African policies and perceptions towards the periphery. First, while the Fourth World is increasingly marginalised in economic terms, certain parts of it may retain some salience for strategic reasons – e.g. Ethiopia and Somalia – at least so long as the superpowers and their associates see the world through bipolar lenses. If the superpower alliances give parts of the periphery a strategic status in the post-detente period then other industrial powers give certain countries – the semi-periphery – an economic advantage in the post-Bretton Woods era.[31]

So, second, inter-imperial rivalries and the emergence of NICs (within as well as outside Africa) may revive the economic opportunities available to some Fourth World states: French economic as well as strategic support of, say, Djibouti or Senegal; Scandinavian support for Guinea-Bissau and Tanzania; Chinese assistance to Tazara; Brazilian involvement in Angola; and Taiwanese help for Malawi and Swaziland fall into this category. Such 'special relationships' do not help all Fourth World states, of course (e.g. Central African Republic after Bokassa or Uganda after Amin). And those that are so helped not only come to rely on new dependencies; they also cannot use them to escape from their structural position at the periphery. In short, such particular links are both tenuous politically and dubious economically; a few leaders may benefit themselves but social peripheralisation and decline are not thereby halted.

In general, however, the structural divergence of periphery and semi-periphery continues in time and can be sustained in theory: their position in the world system is increasingly different as are the characters of their political economies. The state in Africa is no longer homogeneous, if it ever was. Rather, the continent is characterised by a rich diversity of classes and coalitions which come to shape distinctive political economies.

Before proposing one possible way to approach such class relations – contradiction and coalition – I pause to review briefly the few attempts made thus far to apply a more materialist mode of analysis to African cases. Among the few attempts to date to treat the evolution of national political economies from a dynamic class perspective are Giovanni Arrighi's path-breaking work on 'The Political Economy of Rhodesia'[32] and Mahmood Mamdani's rather structuralist *Politics and Class Formation in Uganda.*[33] The comparative collection on *The Political Economy of Africa* edited by Richard

Harris[34] has a very promising introduction, but regrettably the framework is hardly followed by the majority of case studies. The early overview by Basil Davidson which posed the question *Can Africa Survive?*[35] was quite critical but also rather casual; its main ideas are developed in a more coherent and sophisticated manner in his *Africa in Modern History.*[36] Perhaps the most notable and readable synthesis in this genre to date is Irving Markovitz *Power and Class in Africa: An Introduction to Change and Conflict in African Politics,*[37] to be followed by his original collection of *Case Studies in Power and Class in Africa.*[38] Meanwhile, two Longman volumes provide readable, balanced and suggestive versions of the new orthodoxy: Ake *A Political Economy of Africa* and Denis Cohen and John Daniel (eds) *Political Economy of Africa: Selected Readings.*[39] Taken together, this new 'school' of critical African studies advances explanation of both similarities and differences in continental political economies as indicated by Yolamu Barongo:

> [The] dominant characteristics of African politics – such as the intense ethnic and élite conflicts, the recurrent tendencies of instability, the trends towards centralisation of power, the excessive use of power for political repression and the submissive character of the foreign policy of many governments – are explicable, to a great extent, in terms of the material poverty of African countries and the dependent nature of these countries on the operations and manipulations of the international capitalist system.
>
> [In] the study of African problems, the political economy approach, which employs class analysis as its major methodological guide, accompanied by an analysis of historical variables, is superior to the approaches formulated by the so-called Africanists who invariably tend to view African politics through concepts developed in the static tradition of Western bourgeois scholarship.[40]

2 Prognosis: Contradictions and Coalitions

'The essence of neocolonialism is that the state which is subject to it is, in theory, independent and has all the outward trappings of international sovereignty. In reality its economic system and thus its political policy is directed from outside'—Kwame Nkrumah, *Neo-Colonialism: The Last Stage of Imperialism* (London: Heinemann, 1968) p. ix.

'The relationship between a neo-colonialist bourgeoisie and the post-colonial state is clearly of a different order from that which existed between the imperialist bourgeoisie and the colonial state. The class basis of the post-colonial state is therefore complex. It is not entirely subordinate to the indigenous bourgeoisie, in view of the power and influence of the neo-colonial bourgeoisie. Nor is it simply an instrument of any of the latter, which would have the implication that independence is a mere sham. Neither bourgeoisie excludes the influence of the other; and their interests compete'.— Hamza Alavi, 'The State in Post-Colonial Societies: Pakistan and Bangladesh', in Harry Goulbourne (ed.), *Politics and State in the Third World* (London: Macmillan, 1979) p. 41.

'. . . third phase now starting will complete Africa's integration into the world economy. In the coming 50 years this incorporation will take one of two forms: dependent development or revolutionary transformation as part of a network of forces within the world economy as a whole, which will further the transformation to a socialist world system.'—Immanuel Wallerstein, 'The Three Stages of African Involvement in the World Economy', in Peter C. W. Gutkind & Immanuel Wallerstein (eds), *The Political Economy of Contemporary Africa* (Beverly Hills: Sage, 1976) p. 48.

The characters of Africa's political economies have always been heterogeneous despite certain common elements: trade in salt or slaves, pastoral or cultivating economies, hierarchical or egalitarian institutions, etc. On top of pre-colonial differences were added distinctive forms of incorporation (see Amin's typology in the previous chapter, for example) and administration. The combination of pre-colonial and colonial differences generated a variety of nationalist responses – vanguard or mass parties, aristocratic or petty-bourgeois leaderships, populist or socialist ideologies, etc. – which in turn produced various post-independence structures, symbols and situations.[1]

The divergent nature of these inheritances are increasingly apparent and appreciated in 'post-colonial' Africa. The continent is neither static nor homogeneous; rather it exhibits dynamic, dialectical features as do other peripheral social formations. Richard Harris provides a pungent overview of the relationship between colonialism and class which has generated variegated political economies:

> [Colonialism] created a class structure in Africa in which certain traditional strata were reinforced and new strata were developed as a result of the capitalist exploitation fostered by colonial rule . . . the emergence of a series of new classes stemming from the capitalist transformation of African society was by far the most important development during the colonial period.[2]

FROM CLASS COEXISTENCE TO CONTRADICTIONS

The distribution of power and property in Africa continues to change as it has always done, in response to (i) class relations internally and (ii) country and corporate relations externally. These supposedly 'internal' and 'external' factors are, of course, interrelated given the continent's history of incorporation into the world system and continuing transnational linkages. For instance, the prices of salt in pre-colonial, or of petrol in post-colonial, Africa affect the rate and distribution of accumulation internally and externally, intensifying inequalities among both classes and countries.

The initial independence period was marked by an unusual period of growth inside and outside the continent: the fruits of independence seemed to be quite plentiful even if enjoyed by some people more than others. In a 'mixed-sum' situation everyone was able to benefit, albeit unequally: the new 'bureaucratic bourgeoisie' and the crucial labour aristocracy based on import-substitution industries tended to gain at the expense of other workers and peasants. But the realities of this situation were disguised for a time by the general post-independence 'honeymoon' and by the particular expansionist economic climate.

This was the period of 'neo-colonialism' *par excellence,* as characterised by Nkrumah's quote at the beginning of this chapter, in which a very dependent indigenous ruling class – not yet a national bourgeoisie – played a major and privileged part. As Harris suggests, 'This neo-colonial relationship is the product of the transfer of formal political power to a class created by, and dependent upon, Western capitalism.'[3] Its other major feature is the relative affluence and quiescence of organised labour, the second central partner in the neo-colonial coalition of the early 1960s. Arrighi and Saul have noted the origins and opportunities by which the labour aristocracy grew through the spread of 'state capitalism' at least until the early 1970s:

> [The] emergence of a labour aristocracy, with considerable political power, was brought about not only by the pattern of foreign investment but also by the acceptance of a colonial salary structure on the part of independent African governments. The labour aristocracy will therefore continue to use its power in a state-controlled modern sector in order to appropriate a considerable share of the surplus in the form of increasing discretionary consumption.[4]

With the downturn of the global economy and the ending of the import–substitution 'boom', the ability of the labour aristocracy to appropriate surplus has declined. But the determination of the now-established bureaucratic bourgeoisie to accumulate has continued; hence the growing tension between governments and organised labour, a conflict fuelled by inflation which the former has overcome through discretionary increases in salaries and fringe benefits while the latter has been unable to compensate itself as the number of unemployed has undermined its bargaining strength. Marginalisation has diverted the workers' attention towards survival, away from any pretensions of being in the proletarian vanguard. Increasing state control over, or repression of, labour is a further indication of relative power and prosperity in the post-colonial period.

The increasingly antagonistic contradiction between bureaucratic bourgeoisie and labour aristocracy, revealed particularly by the incidence of strikes in the state sector, is just one case of growing class conflicts in Africa. These would have become more apparent in any event as the glamour and growth of independence wore off; they intensified in the seventies because of global and national recession and inflation. The assumptions of the sixties about growth with (some) redistribution – the trickle-down of an era of expansion – gave way to the realities of the seventies – competition for declining surplus in a situation of contraction.

In general, the bourgeoisie – with all its fractions, albeit in differential degrees – was better placed to perpetuate its relative affluence than were other classes as the post-war, post-independence expansion turned into contraction and recession. Its several fractions could use a variety of tactics to achieve the same result – increased salaries and benefits, access to foreign exchange, and control over 'corruption' and/or 'smuggling' – whereas non-bourgeois interests had no countervailing chips to play other than the more dramatic ones of withdrawing labour and/or produce from the market-place. These two rather extreme measures have become quite widespread in the eighties, given the general decline of living standards in the seventies. But this is to anticipate (see Chapter 3).

Before turning to contemporary characteristics of class struggles and strategies I would like to examine general features of class formation and relation in Africa. For as Arrighi and Saul lament, one aspect of the intellectual inheritance of 'oversimplification has been an absence of sufficient differentiation between the component parts of contemporary Africa':

> These similarities and differences become more readily apparent within a framework which focuses upon the various kinds of *uneven development* thrown up by capitalist penetration in Africa. For the underdevelopment of Africa as a whole relative to the industrial centres of the West has been accompanied and mediated by uneven development as between regions, states, tribes, and races *within* Africa itself, and this fact adds important dimensions to the class struggle in Africa and to the character of the resistance of progressive African forces to contemporary imperialism.[5]

TOWARDS A CLASS ANALYSIS OF AFRICA

Despite a growing awareness of the limitations of 'classical' scholarship in Africa, there have been very few attempts to present general or particular analyses of class relations on the continent. Although class formations and relations change over time and among states, and despite the relative newness and plasticity of such social forces in Africa, certain common features can be extracted. And in addition to similar bases, common class coalitions can also be identified for particular types of political economy.

First, all African states include a common set of classes, albeit in differing proportions and degrees: bourgeoisie, petty-bourgeoisie, proletariat, peasantry and a group of marginals: the underemployed and unemployed and migrants. But this typology is relatively uninteresting and unhelpful by itself. What is important is (i) the size and status of each class; (ii) the character of inter-class relations – are they antagonistic or not?; (iii) the degree of cohesion or conflict within each class; and (iv) the position of each country and class in the global system.

First, the size and status of each class varies between time periods and political economies. In no African state is the bourgeoisie dominated by the proletariat or peasantry; but its relative affluence and dominance varies between, say, the restricted accumulation allowed in Ethiopia, Mozambique or Tanzania and the unrestricted *embourgeoisement* characteristic of the Ivory Coast, Nigeria or Zaire. In general, the bigger the national product and the more *laissez-faire* the system the richer (in absolute and relative terms) the bourgeoisie.

But the bourgeoisie is rarely a united class in Africa or elsewhere: depending on the character of the political economy, the bureaucratic, military, comprador, political or national fraction may dominate, with the major contradiction being the relationship between national and transnational or comprador elements, especially in more capitalistic, Third World states. This is a controversial issue in both theory and practice, one dealt with further in Chapter 4. A second class in which a similar tension is apparent is the petty-bourgeoisie which has been increasingly Africanised but within which, at least in certain countries, a national versus foreign conflict remains: Asian traders in Eastern Africa (except post-Amin Uganda, of course) and Lebanese entrepreneurs in West Africa, especially in Liberia and Sierra Leone. There may be a similar schism in the working class too, especially in the more affluent regional centres like Ivory Coast, Kenya and Nigeria, let alone the historic areas of migrant labour like South Africa and Zimbabwe: migrant workers in mining and agriculture in Africa as elsewhere tend to be the lowest paid manual employees unlike better paid and more educated local labourers in manufacturing and service industries. They are always vulnerable to unscrupulous employers and xenophobic governments. Indeed, the only class which, as indicated by the massive 1983 Nigerian expulsion of assorted, especially Ghanaian, aliens, lacks such a national–transnational dimension – except in a limited immediate cross-border sense – is the peasantry which, by definition, is rural, local and traditional: refugees and other migrants, even national ones, are rarely accepted into 'peasant society'. Even the 'informal' sector has transnational elements not only in terms of smuggling but also in terms of trade in 'traditional' goods like leather, ivory and metalwork.

In addition, though, to the national–transnational tension, a major factor in proletarian and peasant classes is their relation to the mode(s) of production. For there is an important 'labour aristocracy' fraction found within the working class while there are, increasingly, big as well as small peasants. In general, the labour aristocracy is of greater importance in the more industrialised economies, especially when workers are under threat because of recession, whereas the big peasantry is most significant in the commodity-exporting economies which have prospered in recent years – Ivory Coast, Kenya and Malawi.

There is, of course, always some difficulty in distinguishing among classes and fractions as change occurs. For example, members of the labour aristocracy may use their relatively high income to reinvest in small shops and workshops, so making steps to move into the petty-bourgeoisie. Similarly, big peasants may use windfall profits from occasional commodity price booms to transform themselves into larger-scale farmers, adjuncts to the black commercial farming fraction of the national bourgeoisie of increasing importance in states like Kenya, Zambia and Zimbabwe. In general, classes are more established and self-conscious in the eighties than in the sixties, partially because the 'neo-colonial' period *per se* has largely ended and partially because they have had time to accumulate and organise. The lumpen-bourgeoisie and the lumpen-proletariat have shed much of their tentativeness and become more viable forces.[6]

Second, the character of class relations – both between and within them – varies over time and between states. In general, there has been a diminution in the power of non-bourgeois forces since independence for two main reasons: (i) the bourgeoisie has become more entrenched and established since the early sixties and less dependent on or interested in non-bourgeois support, as it had been during the nationalist period; and (ii) global recession and inflation have made, especially when intensified through IMF conditionality exports cheaper and imports more expensive, so eroding the economic surplus and foreign exchange of African states (and dominant interests therein).

The only class to maintain and even improve its real income – and then some fractions to a greater degree than others – has been the bourgeoisie; all other classes in differing degrees have suffered relative or absolute losses in their living standards over the last decade. This divergence in the real quality of life between the bourgeoisie and other classes has served to increase social tensions: conflict and repression have grown, particularly since the mid-1970s[7] The nationalist-type of broad social coalition had anyway begun to fragment in the sixties as some received more of the fruits of indpendence than others. In the seventies this 'populist' style of coalition was replaced by more exclusive types: more 'corporatist' and calculating. As Jack Woddis suggests in his useful analysis of the contradictions in and around the national bourgeoisie:

> In all African states, both those which are under progressive leaderships and are cutting away from imperialism, and those which are under reactionary capitalist sections clinging to imperialism, *the internal class struggle is sharpening*. In reactionary states it takes the form of open class battles (strikes, demonstrations, and even the overthrow of governments), ranging from simple economic demands over wages, prices, etc. to the challenging of the whole direction of government policy. In the advanced states, it takes the form of economic and political resistance by the reactionary capitalist sections to the steps of the government and state which are aimed at the further unfolding of the national democratic revolution.[8]

In response to such contradictions, various bourgeois fractions have engineered effective coalitions to resist change, in both state capitalist and state socialist systems.

CLASS COALITIONS IN DIFFERENT POLITICAL ECONOMIES

In the majority of richer NICs in the state capitalist group this coalition has been composed essentially of a more or less balanced 'triple alliance' among national, transnational and state capital, as indicated below. In the majority of poorer LLDCs, both state capitalist and state socialist, the coalition has been less balanced and less stable: state capital dominated by transnational capital often being more important than national. Consequently, the latter coalition – an 'unequal alliance' – is less effective and repressive than the former; non-bourgeois interests are less excluded.

Nonetheless, in both sets of coalition, the bourgeoisie has been, and still remains, dominant. And as Harris notes, at least until quite recently, 'the segment of the bourgeoisie which continues to be the most important in Africa is the bureaucratic bourgeoisie. This element has assumed a central role in the neo-colonial structure and has begun to consolidate its economic relationship with the other segments of the bourgeoisie.'[9] As neo-colonialism fades and a few NICs emerge, so the dominance of the bureaucratic bourgeoisie may be replaced by the national fraction. In the real periphery in decay it may be replaced by the military fraction, and even by petty-bourgeois interests.

In general, however, the bourgeoisie has had little difficulty in maintaining its dominance to date, given its privileged position under both colonialism and neo-colonialism. Moreover, its relationship with labour, especially with the labour aristocracy, has been quite ambiguous and constrained. However, as politics in Africa become zero-sum with the intensifying incidence of recession and inflation so the labour–capital relationship may become more antagonistic.

If labour *v.* capital is one major contradiction in contemporary Africa, the others are within the indigenous bourgeoisie and within the indigenous proletariat. First, intra-bourgeois antagonisms – national *v.* comprador and political *v.* military – are not often so intense or identifiable as those between classes. Nevertheless, given the marginalisation and repression of workers and peasants they may continue to be of considerable salience over the next twenty years as they have been over the previous twenty. And second, in the non-bourgeois group, the co-existence of modes and relations of production mitigates against their political cohesion: region and religion – 'ethnicity' – continue to be powerful pulls.

Two types of intra-bourgeois tensions still mark African political economies. First, the growing antagonisms, particularly within the semi-periphery during a period of protectionism, between national and comprador fractions. And second, the continuing antagonisms, notably within the periphery during a time of contraction, between civilian and military formations. These two sets of contradictions may, of course, overlap – soldiers tend to be more nationalistic – but here I will treat them separately, at least at first. Both, of course, are located within a post-neo-colonial nexus in which extra-African interests are present yet no longer determinant.

NATIONAL *v.* TRANSNATIONAL BOURGEOISIES

The evolution of international capitalism in the post-war world led initially to the creation and expansion of a dependent, *comprador* bourgeoisie in the Third World, one whose potential power increased considerably at independence. In the post-independence period, particularly until the mid-1970s, this fraction used its influence over the new indigenous regimes to improve its transnational position relative to that of its partners in the metropoles: various forms of indigenisation and partial nationalisation spread rapidly. But shifts in the transnational 'balance of power' between external and internal capital were not enough for some indigenous entrepreneurs, particularly those in the semi-periphery in a period of continued expansion. They had outgrown their comprador role and came now to demand relative autonomy . . . a position some had already achieved in pre-colonial times, as in the trans-Sahara trade.

Despite its bourgeois roots, then, at times the national fraction can play a fairly progressive role in association with other classes beyond that of nationalism, particular *vis-à-vis* international capitalism. As Woddis has suggested, in at least the more progressive regimes, because the national bourgeoisie

> desires to see economic expansion and a growth in national production, it understands the need for and supports the idea of the state itself taking the necessary steps to create new national industries. It is the forward-looking section of the bourgeoisie in Africa which, in alliance with the working class, the peasants and revolutionary democrats, is resisting imperialism and struggling against the intrigues of the compromising sections of the bourgeoisie.[10]

But such a role can only be sustained successfully if the nascent national bourgeoisie has already begun to accumulate as in, say, Nigeria in the seventies or South Africa in the fifties. And such a progressive stance tends to be taken only when it is very subordinate; once it has achieved a degree of equality with the transnational or comprador fraction it tends to become more conservative, a partner in a triple alliance *à la* Brazil or South Africa. Its adversary role tends to be transitional unless external interests renew their extractive and interventive activities in a period of expansion.

However, the rise of the national bourgeoisie remains controversial both as a general phenomenon and in particular cases. As Woddis indicated at the beginning of the 1970s:

> The national bourgeoisie in Africa, that is to say that section of the bourgeoisie which is genuinely interested in national independence, national economic growth, the expansion of the internal market, and the creation of national industry, faces very great problems. Generally, it is economically weak, lacks capital, as well as managerial experience and knowledge as regards modern factory production, and has no body of skilled African workers and technicians ready at hand.[11]

However, in the 1980s its position and potential have improved quite dramatically, particularly in relative terms towards other fractions and classes. Already, its presence as a distinctive force separate from branch–plant managers and owners in a range of countries which have achieved a degree of development and industrialisation – Australia, Brazil, Canada, South Africa, etc. – make it a crucial focus of analysis. The case of Brazil is particularly instructive for aspirant African examples; e.g. Algeria, Ivory Coast, Kenya and Nigeria. For Brazil is a case study not only of forced disengagement – its economic foundation was laid during the great depression, so supporting the anti-incorporation preferences of the *dependencia* school – but also of collaboration as well as conflict among bourgeois fractions. As Peter Evans indicates in his analysis of 'dependent development' in Brazil, which is of considerable relevance to analogous African cases:

> Interaction among the dominant elites shaped the transition from classic dependence to dependent development and, in the same way, the interaction of the state, the multinationals, and local capital will shape the response to the contradictions of dependent development.[12]

This formulation of a 'triple alliance' as the social basis of semi-industrialisation at the semi-periphery is of considerable relevance to states like the Ivory Coast, Kenya and Nigeria, particularly the latter with its rapid post-OPEC growth. As Evans comments, 'That the Nigerian case appears suitable to formulations of the triple alliance at all is impressive. In fact, the prospects for Nigeria moving successfully in the direction of the triple alliance seem good.'[13] Through the process of economic 'indigenisation' under the military, Nigerian entrepreneurs have been able to move beyond unequal alliances with multinational corporations and towards shared ownership in a manner reminiscent of Brazil, with profound implications for other African states, especially those in West Africa.[14] To cite Evans again:

> with Nigeria as in Brazil, the local bourgeoisie has not been left out. Given the objective weakness of local private capital in Nigeria and the low likelihood of its making a significant contribution to industrialisation, it would be reasonable to expect a dualistic battle between the state and the multinationals rather than a triple alliance. But, far from being excluded, the local private sector has done extremely well for itself. Relative to its resources, it has probably done better than local capital in Brazil.[15]

The compatibility between foreign and national capital, as in the Brazilian and Nigerian cases, can be sustained providing the world system continues to expand somewhat; if it begins to contract then inter-imperial rivalries will increase and differences between metropole and semi-periphery intensify. As Evans cautions:

> The contradictions between the global rationality of the multinationals and the interests of the local bourgeoisie and the state are seen as potentially resolvable, provided that the overall conditions under which the alliance operates are not too unfavourable to continued capital accumulation in the semi-periphery.[16]

As suggested in Chapter 4, the semi-periphery is likely to be affected by contraction somewhat after the real periphery; but if the recession is long and deep enough the assumptions underlying the 'triple alliance' there may still be eroded.

Arrighi and Saul have been more sceptical about the emergence and role of a national bourgeoisie, but their work on it was initially written over a decade ago when its growth was indeed constrained by global expansion and when nationalist scholarship eschewed such complexities:

> [The] national bourgeoisie will be increasingly incapable of creating growth stimuli independently of international capitalism in the sense that its expansion comes to be almost entirely induced by the complementary growth of the multinational concerns. In consequence, the integration of tropical Africa with the international capitalist system can be assumed to exclude the possibility of a nationalist capitalist pattern of development.[17]

In a period of global contraction, when national bourgeois fractions are already established, the complementarity of national and international bourgeoisies cannot be assumed. Indeed, national capitalism may be the only way for the semi-periphery to grow during a period of protectionism and reindustrialisation in the North. It may be aided in this task of further redressing the 'balance of power' by the intervention of the military fraction in which some of the niceties of transnational negotiation may be disregarded.

CIVILIAN *v.* MILITARY BOURGEOISIES

Despite its overseas training and orientation, paradoxically the army in Africa often perceives itself to be the final arbiter and repository of the 'national interest'. In general, *coups d'état* on the continent have consisted of intra-bourgeois circulation; only occasionally have non-officers from the petty-bourgeoisie seized power successfully, and that under threat from neighbouring bourgeois regimes; namely, Nigeria's resistance towards the two Rawlings coups in Ghana and to Doe's *putsch* in Monrovia. Military regimes typically consider themselves to be objective and nationalistic; they tend to advance the interests of the national bourgeoisie and the working class, at least in their first years in power. Afterwards they may become more repressive and authoritarian, putting their narrowly defined, class-centric 'strategic' interests above all others.[18]

Conceiving of the military in class terms, not as reflective of one class or fraction but rather of several, is an adjunct to Saul's plea for a sensitive neo-Marxist approach to African politics: essentially a struggle within the bourgeoisie. As Saul asks himself, cannot a variety of distinct yet cohesive fractions be identified within

> a class, like the African petty-bourgeoisie, which is at once weak (as any petty-bourgeoisie tends to be), relatively unformed (in the African context), and not yet divided, in any unequivocal manner, into constituent elements diversely rooted in the production process? The result: we find, within the African petty-bourgeoisie, a whole range of 'fractions' which are produced 'in the field of political practice alone'. Moreover, the implications of this formulation are important. For it is precisely such a perspective which, in the realm of theory, can lend to the diverse ethnic, religious, institutional and ideological alignments of Africa's petty-bourgeois politics the *reality* they so clearly possess in practice – while at the same time situating them in such a way as to validate the claims of class analysis to be the crucial key to an understanding of African social formations.[19]

This is a rather different, neo-Marxist perspective from that adopted by Sklar in his non-Marxist analysis of 'class action by the military'.[20] To be sure, soldiers can act as a collective interest group at times. But on other occasions the military may reflect the class divisions within society as a whole: class politics can be played out inside as well as outside the barracks.

When soldiers act for their own particular class reasons, the results may be negative for external countries and corporations; this may be so despite the characteristic conservative orientation of the military. As already noted, military regimes may be quite nationalistic, as during the Mohammed/Obasanjo period in Nigeria. They may also, paradoxically, be unstable. As Saul suggests, Uganda under Amin was an 'unsteady state': 'a dependent social formation which has not given rise to a revolution, but which has nevertheless failed to produce a state adequate to the task of guaranteeing the stable environment necessary for ongoing imperialist exploitation.'[21]

The frequency of political decay, rather than development, often apparent under military regimes, serves to reinforce Shivji's claim that the neo-colonial state is not as reliable as the colonial one for the production of profit for the metropole, even if accumulation proceeds in the periphery itself. Decolonisation has increased the risks to metropolitan investment in the periphery, even when such investment is now protected by state or private partnerships. Co-operation with military rather than civilian fractions does not seem to offer significantly improved prospects for surplus accumulation with confidence. As Saul notes:

> The colonial state provided imperialism with a quite direct and immediate instrument for control in the interests of 'accumulation on a world scale' within the colonial social formation. The post-colonial state, while prone to play a similar role played by its predecessor is something more of an unpredictable quantity in this regard. Unpredictable because of the greater scope for expression given to indigenous elements who now find in the 'independent' state a much more apt target for their activities and a potential instrument for the advancement of their own interests and concerns.[22]

The military is meant to control such 'local difficulties' on behalf of indigenous and metropolitan bourgeoisies, but rarely does so; it alienates rather than unites potential partners in a transnational class coalition.

Instead, the state – particularly in its civilian garb – in peripheral social formations continues to be subject to local pressures. During the nationalist period, opposition was focused on external bourgeois interests, a direction which served to unite disparate internal classes. Now the focus is on the bourgeoisie, internal as well as external; so the opposition is less broad-based. And such struggles tend to flow around the state as the embodiment of such bourgeois interests, as suggested in the last section of this chapter. However, if the African bourgeoisie includes a variety of fractions so too do non-bourgeois classes.

PROLETARIAT, LABOUR ARISTOCRACY AND THE PEASANTRY

Non-bourgeois forces on the continent are not contained within a single homogenous proletariat. Rather, because of the character of Africa's incorporation in the world system, the co-existence of modes of production, and the continuing interest of metropolitan powers, the development of a working class has been delayed – there was minimal industrialisation until independence in all except settler societies – whereas 'peasant society' was encouraged to produce the primary products on which unequal colonial exchange was based. Moreover, those workers that did labour in import–substitution industries in the post-independence period came to constitute a 'labour aristocracy',[23] differentiated from less skilled, poorly paid workers in traditional non-industrial sectors such as commercial farming and government offices. This aristocracy had its position augmented in the first years of independence when local manufacturing grew rapidly; and it has clung onto its relative privilege in the present recession as the size and income of the working class as a whole has shrunk.

Given its origins in post-war international capitalism, the labour aristocracy has tended to be a rather conservative force instead of a progressive proletarian one. Indeed, Arrighi and Saul argue that in the absence of an effective bourgeois class, the labour aristocracy can be the main link with and defence of transnational capital:

> The labour aristocracy owes its very emergence and consolidation to a pattern of investment in which the international corporations play a leading role. The displacement costs involved in the disengagement from international capitalism therefore have to be borne mainly by the labour aristocracy itself.[24]

Any reallocation of the surplus through greater self-reliance would involve, then, a reduction in the consumption habits of this labour aristocracy; hence its resistance to disengagement, whether socialist or not. In other words, the national fraction of the bourgeoisie and the labour aristocracy may be in opposition in their positions towards international capital: the latter resists any move by the former to reduce the operations of multinational corporations from which it believes it benefits. Arrighi and Saul summarise the position of transnational capitalists *vis-à-vis* the national bourgeoisie:

> Other things being equal, given their financial power, greater capital intensity, and scale of operations, they are much less vulnerable to local competition. Secondly, their size and concentration give them a stronger bargaining position at government level. Thirdly, their common and all-pervading interest is to prevent 'nationalist' policies which might tamper with their local operations, irrespective of whether these policies are in favour of a national bourgeoisie, or a racial minority, or the majority of the population.[25]

Generally, however, particularly in the NICs, transnational capital can deal quite readily with national capital: there has been enough growth for both fractions. The labour aristocracy has tended to suffer almost everywhere, meanwhile, for three reasons. First, national capital has come to balance international capital, particularly in the NICs; and it tends to discriminate against relatively high cost labour. Second, the easy stage of import substitution has come to an end almost everywhere; so with rapid population growth the reserve pool of unemployed labour has grown. And, third, the global recession has discouraged foreign investment in the Third World, including Africa. The labour aristocracy is, then, nowhere near as powerful in the eighties as it was in the sixties, when the trade union movement was an important ingredient in the nationalist coalition which underlay most regimes. The decrease in its power has made it vulnerable to the inclusive, corporatist inclinations of contemporary regimes, especially when its income as well as status is under threat from economic decline or decay. And its tacit coalition with comprador elements can hardly save it when the latter are in a tenuous position as colonial-type exchange decreases (as indicated in Table 1·1).

If the proletariat is divided into a labour aristocracy and other workers then the peasantry is equally divided into 'progressive', big peasants and 'traditional' small peasants.[26] This issue of the ability of peasants to accumulate and grow is related to another about their place in peripheral capitalist society. In general, especially in the radical literature, the peasantry is considered to be well integrated into the national, and hence international, capitalist system. Arrighi and Saul articulate this common position:

> [Despite] the existence of some prefigurings of a peasant class in earlier periods, it is more fruitful to view both the creation of an African peasantry, as well as the creation of the present differentiation among African peasantries, as being primarily the result of the interaction between an international capitalist economic system and traditional socio-economic systems, within the context of territorially defined colonial political systems.[27]

By contrast, Goran Hyden has argued, somewhat perversely given prevailing traditional and radical orthodoxies, that 'Africa is the only continent where the peasants have not yet been captured by other social classes'.[28] In his revival of the 'merrie African' myth, allegedly unapproachable by means of 'Western social science', Hyden argues that the 'uncaptured' peasant surplus is *the* cause of African under-development; if more incorporation and exploitation had occurred then development would have been more rapid: 'Development is inconceivable without a more effective subordination of the peasantry to the demands of the ruling class.'[29]

By contrast, most explanations of African underdevelopment are based on the premise that the peasants have been exploited too much rather than too little, and are likely to withdraw from the market rather than seek further integration into it. Their surplus has been extracted all too effectively by the new ruling class, which has learnt how to run a colonial-type state all too well.

Instead of conceiving of the African peasantry as uncaptured and unexploited, Arrighi and Saul argue that it has long since been incorporated; indeed, its incorporation has progressed so far that the processes of proletarianisation and differentiation are proceeding in the rural areas as in the cities:

> [In] certain areas . . . a significant number of African cultivators have moved out of the peasant category and must also be called capitalist farmers. In addition, as the logic of capitalist development has worked itself out in Africa, other peasants have lost their land rights and have been *proletarianised* either in the rural or industrial sectors of the economy. In other words, the further development of capitalism has begun to phase out the very peasantry it first defined and created. Moreover, in most of the continent it is a capitalist route to development that is favoured and insofar as capitalism does have the inherent strength to fully transform African societies, the existence of a peasantry could be viewed all the more as a transitional phenomenon.[30]

Such a position is not only dramatically different from that of Hyden; it also has profound policy implications. Indeed, Arrighi and Saul almost suggest that such perceptions or notions as that of an 'uncaptured peasantry' are not only misleading intellectually; they also coincide with the political preferences of the new ruling class:

> [Even] the relatively unrevolutionised rural economies of tropical Africa are no longer as undifferentiated as these African leaders like to profess. What is clear, therefore, is that the issue of nascent rural class formation and its implications for development cannot be squarely faced, or effective 'long-run' strategies of socialist control and direction developed, with a populist framework of analysis which masks the process of rural change.[31]

Neither rural nor urban political economies remain undifferentiated. In particular, the countryside now includes big and small peasants, with the former striving to become larger-scale 'commercial farmers' and the latter trying to avoid a decline into landlessness. These 'rural' processes have implications for urbanisation and unemployment in the cities. Any development strategy or political ideology has to take, as Arrighi and Saul point out, such distinctions into account: mobilisation is no longer as straightforward as during the nationalist era. Such politics of scarcity reinforce competition for access to, and control over, the state's resources.

THE STATE OF THE STATE

Given the varieties of contradiction and coalition in Africa, the character of the state remains controversial in both orthodox and materialist literatures. The central feature in the continent's colonial inheritance, the state has continued to be the focus of political analysis and *praxis* especially in a period of economic contraction and inflation.

Issa Shivji has presented a useful review of four alternative views of the state in African political economies, preferring the rather subtle formulation discussed in the introduction, the one which is most compatible with the ideas presented here of post-colonial coalitions in a post-industrial world:

> In the neo-colonial state, state power rests in the hands of a local class or classes . . . [who] have their own interests arising from the place they occupy in social production, which in the longer run coincide with the interests of imperialism as a whole. In a neo-colonial situation, the inter-imperialist rivalries come to have full weight because the various factions and classes in the local state power forge alliances with different imperialist powers in line with their own interests.[32]

This neat integration or juxtaposition of 'internal' contradictions and 'external' rivalries nicely cuts through established debates about the dependent and overdeveloped state. Rather, Shivji conceives of the state as neither free nor determined; neither autonomous nor captured. Rather, it is simply the focus or locus of various forms of indigenous and foreign interests and conflicts, an increasingly disparate set of coalitions in contemporary Africa.

Shivji rejects, therefore, three alternative approaches. First, he is critical of 'Soviet determinism', the assumption that all states will go through the stage of a 'non-capitalist state'[33] or the 'state of the entire people' en route to 'real' socialism. Second, he is dubious about the 'independent Marxists' like John Saul[34] and Roger Murray who still conceive of classes as being in formation; they imply, logically, that the state is also unformed and so open to manipulation by particular fractions in the direction of socialism. Finally, third, Shivji reserves his severest criticism for a group of ex-Dar es Salaam 'comrades': the 'vulgar' or 'structuralist' Marxists like Dan Nabudere[35] and Yash Tandon who see but one global oligarchy in which the place of local classes is merely comprador. For them national finance capitalisms are an impossibility; there is but one metropolitan bourgeoisie and so one global class struggle. As indicated in his quotation at note 8 in the Introduction, Shivji rejects such a simplistic, structuralist viewpoint, preferring a more sophisticated and nuanced approach which links local and global contradictions and coalitions.

Shivji's position is clearly closer to the neo-Marxism of Saul than the 'super-Marxism' [36] of Nabudere. Yet he goes some way beyond the somewhat hesitant and tentative formulation of the former, as captured by this statement:

> [It] is the petty-bourgeoisie which will be in direct control of the post-colonial state, this 'over-developed' state being, in turn, an important prize, well-suited to arbitrate for aspirant Africans in terms and methods of capital accumulation in the new economies as well as the uses to which various surpluses and scarce resources are to be put. This, then, is the core of a realistic class analysis of contemporary Africa. What cannot be said with the same degree of certainty is who among the petty-bourgeoisie-in-formation will relieve such control of the state.[37]

The clear centrality of the state to the process of accumulation has led Richard Sklar to mistaken political power for economic position. In his non-Marxist 'class' analysis, Sklar emphasises control over the state as a goal in itself rather than as an instrumental, intermediate value. To be sure, control over the state apparatus is important throughout the continent, especially so in state socialist rather than capitalist systems; i.e. in Tanzania rather than in Nigeria. But the 'silent class struggle' is still ultimately about economic rather than political position. Hence the unacceptability of Sklar's formulation that

> class relations are determined by relations of power. Class formation is a consequence of determinants that are specifically political as well as economic. However 'dependent' or 'extroverted' the economy of an under-developed country may be, the autonomy of its bourgeoisie may yet be firmly established upon a foundation of indigenous political organisation.[38]

Access to, or control over, the state is increasingly sought as a means to sustain lifestyle and accumulate capital not merely as a quest for status and visibility; this is particularly so in hard-hit states at the periphery. Moreover, as peripheral social formations become more complex so struggles to capture the state become less decisive.

Given its origins in both colonialism and nationalism, and given the complexities of class formations and relations on the continent, nowadays the state in Africa is rarely dominated by one class or fraction, although at times one man may come to symbolise it. Rather, as Hamza Alavi suggests:

> The state in the post-colonial society is not the instrument of a single class. It is relatively autonomous and it mediates between the competing interests of the three propertied classes, namely the metropolitan bourgeoisies, the indigenous bourgeoisies and the landed classes, while at the same time acting on behalf of them all to preserve the social order in which their interests are embedded, namely the institution of private property and the capitalist mode as the dominant mode of production.[39]

This formulation is particularly relevant for capitalist states at the semi-periphery. In more state capitalist or state socialist states, state capital and, sometimes, non-bourgeois interests may also play an important part in co-directing the state.

Having sketched out an alternative approach to coalitions and contradictions in the African political economy, I turn in the second half of this volume to a somewhat more speculative look at what this means to Africa in the mid-term future, emphasising substructural as well as superstructural features. The present crisis has profound implications for the continent over the next decade or two in terms of both projections and policy choices, or lack thereof: will the crisis constitute a conjuncture or not?

Part II

The African Conjuncture

3 Prospective: Minimal Growth and Uneven Development

'Men make their own history, but they do not make it just as they please; they do not make it under circumstances chosen by themselves, but under circumstances directly encountered, given and transmitted from the past. The tradition of all the dead generations weighs like a nightmare on the brain of the living. And just when they seem engaged in revolutionising themselves and things, in creating something that has never yet existed, precisely in such periods of revolutionary crisis they anxiously conjure up the spirits of the past to their service and borrow from them names, battle cries, and costumes in order to present the new scene of world history in this time-honoured disguise and this borrowed language.'—Karl Marx, *18th Brumaire of Louis Bonaparte,* p. 398.

'If . . . our interests are to keep our countries as neo-colonies and to perpetuate the existing class exploitation and domination, then we should teach and encourage bourgeois social science. If, on the other hand, we want to change African countries from neo-colonies to independent and self-reliant nations . . . we must employ the science of dialectical materialism in our teaching of political science.'—Wang Metuge, 'Class Interests in the Teaching of Political Science in African Universities', in Yolamu Barongo (ed.), *Political Science in Africa: a critical review* (London: Zed, 1983) p. 54.

'["Neo-colonialism"] . . . is taken to explain everything at the political level without any sustained effort to examine neo-colonialism itself and what it actually means at the level of the development of productive forces, social relations of production, class contradictions, and so on . . . For political scientists studying the politics of peripheral capitalist societies it is therefore crucial to focus on the dynamics of capitalist accumulation on the world scale as it affects the development of the peripheral formation. Close study must be devoted to the dynamics of incorporation and penetration by international capital and its interaction with processes of accumulation and class formation at the local level.'—Bjorn Beckman, 'Political Science and Political Economy', in Yolamu Barongo (ed.), *Political Science in Africa: a critical review* (London: Zed, 1983) pp. 109–10.

The theme of the first half of this study has been the need to go beyond orthodoxy in both analysis and theory: established notions of class and contradiction must be transcended if central modes and relations of production in Africa's variegated and divergent political economies are to be identified, abstracted and explained. As already noted, this rather ambitious task – which, as this second part indicates, is already under way – involves going beyond both development and dependence, neo-colonialism and nationalism towards a more sophisticated and subtle form of neo-Marxism in which a range of classes and fractions, contradictions and coalitions are recognised. Such a perspective also requires the abstraction of several levels of analysis, especially the global and national, and several periods of history, particularly the colonial, post-colonial and post-neo-colonial.

In short, several pervasive and persuasive myths about Africa need to be discarded if we are to advance beyond rhetoric: neither idealistic modernisation theories nor simplistic Marxist dichotomies serve to enhance the economic and intellectual development of the continent. Rather a historically rooted, sociologically informed and globally situated study of ambiguities and ironies within African political economies is essential if explanation is to be accurate and prescription is to be appropriate. This chapter attempts to integrate some of the concepts proposed in the first half – fractions and coalitions as well as countries and contradictions – as a means to improve analysis and inform *praxis*.

AFRICA'S MARGINALISATION IN A POST-EXPANSION GLOBAL ECONOMY

Although Africa in a post-detente period may once again be more crucial in the global military balance, its economic marginality has been further advanced and advertised by the demise of OPEC (see Tables 1·1 and 3·1). Indeed, the brief period of growth for a few oil-exporting countries which resulted from the dramatic escalation in the price of petroleum in the mid-1970s served only to (i) disguise the long-term trend towards concentration for all but a few political economies; (ii) increase the immediate crisis for the majority of states; and (iii) exacerbate embryonic intellectual and ideological differences on the continent. The transitional character of the OPEC decade, 1972–83, became all too apparent in subsequent years: the seemingly ineluctable trend towards the continent's marginalisation (see Table 3·2).

Despite interminable and inconclusive debates about a New International Economic Order, at the level of diplomacy and ideology a new international division of labour *has,* in fact, been evolving at the level of production both globally and nationally.[1]

TABLE 3·1 *Projections of selected commodity exports outside the region under the historical trends scenario*

	1980		*2008*		
	Quantity (thousands of tons)	*Value at 1980 prices (million $)*	*Quantity (thousands of tons)*	*Value at 1980 prices (million $)*	*Average annual growth rate (percentage)*
Cash crops					
Coffee	957.0	3 177.2	2 324.9	7 718.7	3.2
Cocoa	837.0	1 944.3	1 568.8	3 642.7	2.3
Cotton	622.0	2 101.7	3 098.7	10 470.5	5.9
Tobacco	148.0	340.4	245.2	563.5	1.8
Tea	177.0	658.4	483.3	1 251.7	3.6
Minerals					
Copper	980.5	2 137.5	1 578.6	3 441.3	1.6
Iron ore	26.2	461.0	36.6	644.2	1.2
Bauxite	13.1	539.7	19.3	795.2	1.4
Energy					
Crude oil	279.0	66 067.2	254.3	60 147.2	−0.3
Natural gas	13.6	2 448.0	61.1	10 998.0	5.1

SOURCE ECA, *ECA and Africa's Development,* 49, and secretariat projections, 1983.

TABLE 3·2 *Principal merchandise exports of sub-Saharan Africa*

	1976–78 average			
			Principal exporter	
	Value (millions of dollars)	Percentage share of Sub-Saharan African exports	Country	Percentage share of exports from Sub-Saharan Africa
Fuels				
Petroleum	11 502	43.5	Nigeria	95.5
Mineral and metals				
Copper	1589	6.0	Zambia	54.0
Iron ore	432	1.6	Liberia	67.9
Bauxite	188	0.7	Guinea	95.1
Phosphate rock	140	0.5	Togo	58.6
Manganese ore	120	0.5	Gabon	85.7
Zinc	79	0.3	Zaire	57.7
Tin	59	0.2	Nigeria	43.8
Lead	20	0.1	Namibia	63.9
Food and beverages				
Coffee	2838	10.7	Ivory Coast	22.5
Cocoa	1882	7.1	Ghana	34.5
Sugar	432	1.6	Mauritius	48.5
Tea	245	0.9	Kenya	57.7
Groundnuts	194	0.7	Sudan	52.1
Groundnut oil	177	0.7	Senegal	80.8
Beef	78	0.3	Botswana	43.4
Palmoil	58	0.8	Ivory Coast	71.4
Bananas	45	0.2	Ivory Coast	32.8
Maize	30	—		
Non-food				
Timber	680	2.6	Ivory Coast	47.4
Cotton	651	2.5	Sudan	46.0
Tobacco	290	1.1	Zimbabwe	47.8
Rubber	128	0.5	Liberia	47.5
Sisal	50	0.2	Tanzania	52.8
All other exports	4553	17.2		
Total exports of Sub-Saharan Africa	26 458	100.0	Nigeria	41.5

SOURCE World Bank, *Agenda for Action*, 152.

Whilst the NIEO issue has been characterised by inter-state negotiation over rules and relations, the actual division has taken on its own momentum as corporations and countries have successively diversified and concentrated production. At the height of the post-war Bretton Woods order and of the African nationalist ferment, companies, in a period of decentralisation, encouraged import-substitution industrialisation. But when national markets and conditions deteriorated initially they welcomed partial nationalisation or indigenisation and subsequently they neglected or abandoned their African investments. The continent is now full of old-fashioned, inappropriate and under-utilised technology, with profound implications for national development and class dialectics. In only a handful of states did the local economy or national bourgeoisie ensure continued capital and techological inflows once international expansion was succeeded by contraction. Elsewhere, foreign exchange constraints, infrastructural deficiencies and inadequate demand led to low productivity and expensive products, a trend unrelieved by the lower real cost of energy from the early 1980s onwards.

Africa's marginalisation has both structural and superficial features, then, which need to be distinguished. The *superficial* features are quite familiar and relate directly to the NIEO agenda: growth, industry, prices, exchange and debt (see Tables 3·3, 3·4 and 3·5). They also get reflected in rhetoric and dialogues: continual demands for attention, restructuring and redistribution. Indeed, a dialectic of pathos may be found in Africa's growing marginality and increasing assertiveness: neglect and *triage* are rather awesome prospects for dependent and insecure ruling classes.[2]

TABLE 3·3 *Balance of payments of developing Africa (billions of US dollars)*

	1970	*1975*	*1978*	*1979*	*1980*
Exports (f.o.b.)	12.3	34.9	48.0	68.2	92.8
Imports (f.o.b.)	−10.3	−35.8	−51.2	−58.0	−72.7
Trade balance (f.o.b.)	2.0	−0.9	−3.2	10.2	20.1
Net services and private transfers	−3.4	−8.5	−11.8	−14.1	−15.9
Balance on current account	−1.4	−9.4	−15.0	−3.9	4.2
Official transfers (net)	1.2	2.5	2.6	2.7	2.4
Capital (net)	2.2	6.1	10.4	11.5	8.8
Net errors and omissions	−0.7	−1.5	−0.6	−3.3	−2.2
Total change in reserves	−1.3	2.3	2.8	−7.0	−13.2

SOURCE ECA, *Silver Jubilee Anniversary Meeting,* April–May 1983, p. 31.

TABLE 3·4 *Terms of trade and export trends, selected African countries, by export category*[a]

	Average annual rate of growth					
	Purchasing power of exports		*Net barter terms of trade*		*Export volume*	
Category	*1961–70*	*1970–9*	*1961–70*	*1970–9*	*1960–70*	*1970–9*
1. Oil exporters[b]	7.7	12.6	1.2	14.7	7.1	−2.0
2. Mineral exporters[c]	11.1	−7.7	6.5	−7.1	4.6	−0.7
3. Other primary exporters[d]	4.9	1.1	1.0	2.9	4.7	−2.1
Subtotal, oil importers (Categories 2 + 3)	7.6	−2.7	3.4	−1.5	4.7	−1.5
Total Sub-Saharan Africa	7.6	1.0	2.9	2.5	5.3	−1.6

[a] Country group averages are weighted by value of country merchandise exports in 1970.
[b] Angola, Congo, and Nigeria.
[c] Liberia, Mauritania, Niger, Sierra Leone, Togo, Zaire, and Zambia.
[d] Benin, Cameroon, C.A.R., Chad, Ethiopia, Ghana, Ivory Coast, Kenya, Madagascar, Malawi, Mali, Rwanda, Senegal, Somalia, Sudan, Tanzania, Uganda, and Upper Volta.

SOURCE UNCTAD, *Handbook of International Trade and Development Statistics,* 1980 and World Bank, *Agenda for Action,* 18.

TABLE 3·5 *Actual and projected sub-Saharan African debt-service ratios (per cent)*

Category	*1977*	*1978*	*1980*	*1985*	*1990*
Oil importers	8.4	10.6	15.8	17.6	19.8
Low income	8.4	10.4	19.2	9.5	19.9
Middle income	8.1	10.1	13.6	16.2	19.3
Oil exporters	1.8	3.3	3.5	4.6	4.1

SOURCE World Bank, *Agenda for Action,* 129.

The *structural* features are, however, less apparent and more profound: Africa's changing place in the effective international division of labour. The continent's incorporation into the world economy was in response to the metropole's need – or, more accurately, the need of some classes and companies in the metropole – for certain materials and markets. Even before independence, changes in the global economy had produced significant shifts in the patterns of such needs – from palm and other natural oils to petroleum and from consumer products to semi-manufactured goods. But the very success of the Bretton Woods order served to disguise structural changes and independence honeymoons and the Vietnam War further camouflaged trends.

The dislocation and recession of the mid-1970s were in some ways inevitable given previous growth and expansion.[3] Their intensity and persistence were quite shocking, nonetheless. Suddenly it became clear just how vulnerable most African economies and regimes were once old assumptions about the 'neocolonial nexus' were discarded:[4] sisal and copper were no longer needed in a world of synthetic fabrics, glassfibre communications or plastic piping, while even accommodating rulers had little place when external entrepreneurs were disinterested. Moreover, as the price and production of primary commodities fell so surplus extraction by the post-colonial state became problematic: the first generation of nationalist leaders lost their milieu and their means.[5] As the conjuncture of global recession and national austerity became apparent, the fractions of the ruling class clamoured to preserve their privilege and to find a new place for themselves. I turn to such a new scramble in Africa after an overview of new inequalities and ambiguities.

FROM ANTICIPATED EQUALITY TO PROJECTED INEQUALITY

The ideological and intellectual assumptions and orientations of the classic African nationalist movements were profoundly liberal as well as externally oriented: the colonial powers were basically reasonable and honourable so transition to independence was inevitable and an expanding world system would provide the engine of growth. However, in the event, not only were white settlers to prove to be somewhat less than generous but international exchange was neither so accessible nor as automatic as had been believed. Just as external difficulties arose so internal problems proliferated for the continent: countries and classes were not as equal as had been presumed. The honeymoon period was shattered first by military coups and then by economic crises. By the 1980s the first, idealistic generation of leaders had been superseded by subsequent chastened and pragmatic rulers – or, in a few cases, authoritarian and vengeful tyrants: national integration and development were replaced as motifs by personal survival and affluence for both benign and malign presidents.

The apparent divergencies of post-independence Africa have produced a series of dialectics. Central to these are a set of intra- and inter-state antagonisms on the continent along with several patterns of extra-continental connections directed towards more industrialised capitalist and socialist systems. This mix of class and country relations are, of course, interconnected, not in any mechanistic manner characteristic of vulgar neo-colonial or dependence perspectives, but rather through a series of dialectical relations. In the previous part an overview or framework for these intricate linkages was proposed, with the rest of the chapter focusing on some salient implications of such relations. The links include intra- as well as inter-state connections of conflict and co-operation involving sets of coalitions as well as antagonists. It is within such situations (i) that the clash of fractions already outlined takes place and (ii) that alternative development strategies are designed.

POLITICS OF PRODUCTION: NEW FORCES AND FRACTIONS

The new scramble for or in Africa is not so much among external companies and countries (except, perhaps, for access to the few NIC markets when OECD members are in a recessionary and competitive cycle) as among internal classes and fractions. The old inclusive coalitions of the nationalist era – a period of real and perceived growth – have been superseded by exclusive alignments competing for the minimal increments and opportunities still available. As already indicated, these are to be found particularly in state and military bourgeois formations attempting to curb the relentless downward pressure on their living standards and expectations. It is within this nexus that the dynamics of regime changes and corrupt practices are to be found: survival strategies for abandoned fractions in hard times.[6]

In the previous chapter I suggested an outline within which African political economy can be situated and analysed, with particular emphasis on coalitions and contradictions, a rather *static* structure.

Here I hope to develop this framework further by examining the *dynamics* of such social formations with particular emphasis on (i) their role in production as well as in politics and distribution, and (ii) their place in the broader global division of labour. These two phenomena are, of course, interrelated: as so much production in Africa involves external inputs – particularly capital and technology – and exports, this leads to vulnerability towards external demand, competition, exchange rates and debt ratios. So it is not only some African *products* which have become marginal in the world system but also certain African *producers:* the decline of cocoa production and price in Ghana has affected not only the national economy and polity but also the balance between farmers and other formations, as well as that within the bourgeoisie, between bureaucrats, professionals and soldiers.[7]

And, to be sure, there is a dialectical relationship between global and national political economies: changes in social relations impact upon production as well as vice versa. Questions of cause and effect, of independent and dependent variables, cannot be separated, of course, from theory and policy: while materialist scholars now focus on modes and relations of production at the level of substructure, more 'bourgeois' or modernisation perspectives still treat social and political relations at the level of superstructure. Here I attempt to incorporate elements from both sets of factors, whilst recognising the centrality and primacy of relations of production over those of politics and distribution. The contemporary conjuncture is, clearly, one of *praxis* as well as of production and opposition.

Furthermore, the marginalisation of some African producers as well as products cannot be separated from the exclusiveness of both national regimes and transnational corporations: one-party states and global companies manipulate social linkages to their own advantage. Exclusive regimes discard subversive or subordinate groups whilst international businesses link up with or ignore indigenous companies and entrepreneurs according to their own interests and imperatives. And such concerns may be shared between regimes and companies – a reconceptualisation of 'neo-colonialism' – as they come to re-define their common interests, through processes of 'indigenisation' and 'nationalisation': both seek to exploit peasants and proletariats while constructing infrastructures in the cities to further external incorporation and internal embourgeoisement. Indeed, their intra-class interests may also diverge as over the distribution of capital, control and direction. However, while tensions may exist within the 'transnational bourgeoisie', such disagreements are minor compared with the contradictions between it and African non-bourgeois elements: inter- rather than intra-class antagonisms. And as national growth has slowed or reversed, so class differences and disagreements have intensified: the zero-sum character of African political economies has become more apparent in a period of recession and contraction.

Paradoxically, as so many African economies have gone into decline, the attendant marginalisation of the middle classes, who concentrate now on survival rather than on professional roles, the informal sectors – what are known as the 'black market' or sector in 'white' metropolitan economies – have experienced a revival. The days of importing machines and parts at will are past; only roadside mechanics and creative technicians can now hope to maintain the national fleet or plant. Moreover, as the logic of commodity exports has evaporated so peasants have returned to food production, at least for themselves if not for the cities. The breakdown of many national economies has led, then, to the revival of traditional practices and skills. Not that these can generate by themselves sufficient capital for self-reliant development. But at least they do point to 'another way'[8] aside from imitative lifestyles and technologies.

The characteristic breakdown of 'modern' production in African economies has led, dialectically, to the demise of state structures and social relations. Institutions developed for the transition to independence now lack constituencies as the import–export sectors essential to extroverted production have decayed; another reason, incidentally, for going beyond orthodox, state-centric analysis of the African reality. And post-war social relations, especially those between capital and labour, parastatals and workers, have fragmented as their *raison d'être* has been undermined.[9] Africa always lacked productive capacity; and much of what it had now lies either under-utilised or idle. Established connections among factors of production exist in disarray as new forms of production – more indigenous, less sophisticated, yet quite relevant – are established through social crises: an indigenous form of 'networking'. The post-colonial state has been superseded by the post-neo-colonial state, whose form is presently embryonic if not anarchic.[10]

The 'corporatist' response to many regimes is, then, an attempt to capture what little surplus is created in economies in decline: the bureaucratic, political and military fractions of the bourgeoisie seek to prop up their vulnerable positions and tenuous lifestyles by

TABLE 3·6 *Structure of expenditure on GDP, 1960–80 (in percentage shares)*

		Private consumption	*Government consumption*	*Total consumption*	*Savings*	*Investment*
Major oil exporters	1960	79.3	12.6	91.9	8.1	23.1
	1980	59.2	20.3	79.5	20.5	33.5
Non-oil exporters	1960	72.7	13.5	86.2	13.8	13.8
	1980	64.6	18.6	83.3	16.7	18.5
Least developed countries	1960	79.1	10.3	89.4	10.6	10.6
	1980	75.2	16.4	91.6	8.4	16.0
Developing Africa	1960	74.4	13.3	87.6	12.4	16.1
	1980	62.4	19.3	81.7	18.3	24.9

SOURCE ECA, *Silver Jubilee Meeting*, April–May 1983.

excluding other claimants to the contracting national pie (on the growth of government versus private consumption everywhere see Table 3·6).[11] Conversely, those excluded seek, often through corruption and crime, to perpetuate their access to foreign exchange and inputs. Just as the national infrastructure is being neglected in post-Bretton Woods Africa as the ruling class concentrates on its own embourgeoisement, so the national polity has gone into a period of decay as personal gain is typically (and rationally) placed ahead of collective good.[12]

If the majority of states and peoples in the periphery are now preoccupied by survival rather than by accumulation, a few in the semi-periphery have participated in the more familiar politics of fractional competition. Instead of the misleading politics of populism,[13] the latter have perpetuated faith in developmentalism; they have eschewed authoritarianism and extended nationalism. Despite cyclical shifts and periods of austerity, faith has so far been maintained in the Ivorian miracle and the Nigerian dream. Thus class relations in such formations remain more orthodox, with fractional conflicts within the bourgeois being more salient than class contradictions between it and the proletariat or peasantry.[14] Yet in both periphery and semi-periphery, given the buffeting of global forces, the time for complacency is long past; and the efficacy of established strategies will not last forever, especially in corporatist systems under pressure. Yet Samir Amin warns that the prospects for any such change – for seizing the chance along the lines indicated in the conclusion – will not extend indefinitely: '[The] deadlock . . . will . . . continue . . . until new social forces appear, open to the future rather than dominated by the past.'[15]

Reformism is not yet seen to be an impossibility in Africa despite the incidence of significant social 'revolutions' in Algeria, Angola, Ethiopia, Mozambique and Zimbabwe; the incidence of black markets in all variety of goods along the West African coast, for example, has not yet led either to the collapse of political economies such as those of Ghana or Guinea or to the articulation of novel developmental responses based on the recognition and incorporation of such resilient structures.

Pragmatism still prevails whether in national strategy or in personal survival. It is, of course, just five years or so since the structural rather than cyclical changes of the North began to impinge on the continent; there still remains a vestigial hope that the combination of recession, inflation and contraction is but a passing phase. The full impact of conservation and reorientation in the advanced industrialised states has not yet been felt by Africa's leaders and peoples, cushioned or conditioned as they are by 'internationalist' rhetoric and resources.

But structural changes in the global economy will yet affect political and social as well as economic relations: in a post-Bretton Woods era, the North is relatively disinterested in interfering, except for great power 'strategic' politics; and even that is proving too expensive and unpredictable for regular adoption. To be sure, some emergency assistance will be forthcoming in terms of food and foreign exchange, but the continuous structural connection has withered as a result of energy crises and the combination of inflation and unemployment. The pressures for 'reindustrialisation' amongst the OECD states, advocated especially by organised labour, have changed the balance in North–South relations at the levels of countries, classes and companies.

If the rationale of comprador fractions is thereby undermined, the potential of national capital, military bourgeoisies, proletarian demands and peasant pressures are all enhanced, reinforced by reformist rhetoric from the Brandt Commission and the ECA. Hence the shake-up in African political economies as post-nationalist elements cling to power and privilege while post-neo-colonial forces begin to flex muscles. All this in a world system characterised by redefinitions of the international division of labour; the African periphery is further marginalised while the semi-periphery attempts to maintain its intermediate status, even seeking to 'graduate' into the charmed circle of the OECD. The continuing evolution of social forces within Africa and the world reinforce such tendencies towards country and class divergence. After all, the triple alliance does require the collaboration of multinational capital, national capital and the local state;[16] in the 1980s, the former may be disinterested, national capital may be in decline, and the latter may be in decay. Only in the semi-periphery might a favourable environment exist for such a conjuncture of forces; and even there it is problematic given competitiveness among multinational corporations, the tenuousness of national capital and the uncertainty of the local regime.

CLASS BASES OF AFRICAN IDEOLOGIES AND POLICIES

The transformation of class relations in Africa attendant upon changes in national and global political economies has affected debates about development strategies, their definition and implementation. The sharpening of antagonisms within and between classes has been reflected in intensifying disagreements over what is to be done. Given the decline in surplus and the competition for access, tensions over resources and responses have increased with intensifying class consciousness about divergent interests. Instability and uncertainty over the conception and execution of national policies and plans reflect this new volatility as reflected in, say, disagreements in Zambia over dependence on copper and relations with South Africa,[17] or in Nigeria over dependence on petroleum and relations with the advanced industrialised states.[18] At the present time, the intense yet sporadic continental discussion about alternative development directions and strategies, noted in subsequent chapters, is symptomatic of divergent interest between and within countries.

The current debate over self-reliance and self-sustainment leads to divided responses along the lines of countries, organisations and classes, both within and between states inside and outside Africa. Already, some *countries* have moved in intent and (even if to lesser degree) in practice towards self-reliance – such as Benin, Somalia and Tanzania – while others continue to encourage external incorporation – despite the new imponderables of 'neo-colonialism' – for example, Egypt, Ivory Coast and Kenya. In general, the more peripheral political economies are more predisposed towards disengagement than the less peripheral, reflecting in part their own 'national interests'.[19]

Likewise, the more peripheral *classes* are also predisposed towards disengagement rather than dependence, having benefited minimally over the last two decades from an inheritance of incorporation. If the bourgeoisie in general prefers further linkage to perpetuate its association with, and access to, 'international' lifestyles then the proletariat and peasantry, particularly in a period of impoverishment and having apparently little to gain from external connections, tend to identify with self-reliance. This neat dichotomy does not always hold, however. In particular, two fractions already identified (see previous chapter) are inclined to break ranks with their classes: the national bourgeoisie tends to dissociate itself from an outward-oriented strategy because of its ongoing fights with other fractions, and the labour aristocracy, given its connections with international business and unions, still advocates an external orientation despite the overall position of the proletariat.[20]

Such a dichotomy over extroverted versus introverted preferences can also split ministries, parastatals and non-state actors in Africa: obviously oil and commodity marketing boards or agencies insist on an outward orientation whereas national banks and development institutions espouse more autocentric approaches. Finally, extra-African countries, companies and non-state actors may also be divided into those favouring self-reliance versus those preferring a transnational emphasis. While most multinational manufacturers encourage 'free' trade and investment, the banks, with exposed debts, may advocate self-reliance as a means to facilitating repayment; and many non-governmental organisations like churches, volunteer and charitable agencies may encourage it as a means to satisfy BHN and to maximise individual potential.[21]

Not all forms of either extroversion or introversion are compatible, of course. More radical, self-reliant states, for instance, may discourage sub-national or regional self-reliance as indicated by, say, Ethiopia and Tanzania, respectively. And more conservative, extroverted economies, particularly the NICs, may compete for regional and global markets, such as the tension between Nigeria and the Ivory Coast over ECOWAS and oil consumers. And if regimes compete, so too do classes and fractions within them, particularly bourgeois and proletarian fractions whether represented in ministries, parastatals and interest groups or not.

The balance of forces among such formations is a function of global as well as continental and national conditions. The hegemony of comprador bourgeois and labour aristocratic fractions was assured after independence as the expansion of international and national economies coincided with the widespread adoption of import-substitution industrialisation. However, the inevitable contradictions and demise of such a strategy, even when it was extended for a few years amongst some 'middle' powers through a transition to export-led manufacturing,[22] eroded such hegemony and made the established comprador–labour aristocracy alliance vulnerable to a new national bourgeoisie–informal sector coalition. This transition was accelerated and intensified, of course, by the economic shocks and crises of the mid-1970s – 'The great boom ended in 1972–4. It became a myth with great speed, enshrined in a revival of the fifties rocking generation, in the nostalgia of the sixties generation'[23] – but was predictable given the balkanised, competitive character of the African economy.

Hence the support within certain countries for the *Lagos Plan of Action* if it is seen as a means to advance the hegemony of the national bourgeoisie at the expense of comprador elements. Further, any emphasis on relevant, renewable technologies will appeal to certain fractions of labour by contrast to the peasantry, which is still locked into commodity production for export as favoured by the World Bank. The demise of import substitution has led the Bank to advocate a return to agricultural exportation rather than an advance towards more appropriate patterns of production for popular markets (on the imperative of improved domestic food production see Tables 3·7 and 3·8); e.g. buses and bicycles rather than personal automobiles, and local grains and beers rather than 'cornflakes', white bread and lager:

> Import substitution can be a sound policy and most industrialisation has started on that basis. But in many African countries it has

TABLE 3·7 *FAO indices of agricultural production in developing Africa*

	Growth rates			
	1961–70	*1971–75*	*1975–80*	*1971–80*
Food production *(per capita)*	–	−1.6	−1.1	−1.1
Agricultural production	2.7	1.0	2.2	1.6
Forestry production (roundwood)	4.0	−0.2	2.4	1.2
Fish production	7.3	2.2	4.8	4.1

SOURCE ECA, *Silver Jubilee Anniversary Meetings,* April–May 1983, p. 7, based on FAO, *State of Food and Agriculture* 1974, 1978, 1980.

TABLE 3·8 *Value of cereal imports by developing Africa* (millions of US dollars)

	1961	*1970*	*1980*
North Africa	206.1	211.7	2596.2
West Africa	61.3	149.8	1079.5
Central Africa	17.5	59.3	238.2
Eastern and Southern Africa	43.0	111.3	780.4
Developing Africa	327.9	532.1	4694.3

SOURCES ECA, *Silver Jubilee Anniversary Meetings* April–May 1983, p. 7 and FAO, *Trade Yearbook,* 1967, 1971, 1973, 1976 and 1980.

> been badly implemented . . . For countries that have nearly completed the first stages of import substitution, such as Kenya, Ivory Coast and Tanzania, few import substitution opportunities exist based on the internal market.[24]

The imperative of economic restructuring, and so a realignment of social forces, is a result not only of internal contradictions but also of (interrelated) external constraints: protectionism in the North produced by recession and inflation has closed off possible markets for manufactured and agricultural products even before they were really penetrated. This combined with growing Northern disinterest in many African products or sources – why struggle to get iron-ore out of Guinea or aluminium out of Ghana when they can be more easily, even if not more cheaply, produced elsewhere? – has introduced an element of inevitability into Africa's rediscovery of itself. Already Africa may be too late to insert its own interests into the new *de facto* international division of labour.

The designation of the present decade as that for 'industrial development in Africa'[25] is, then, both paradoxical and fortuitous: paradoxical as it occurs when industrial production, miniscule though it may be, is declining on the continent, yet fortuitous because if the continent is ever to become more self-reliant and integrated it needs a broad-scale manufacturing capacity along with an internal source of supply of industrial inputs. But the prerequisites for a successful execution of any industrial strategy – stability and integration – are elusive precisely because of the continent's underdevelopment: a real Catch-22 contradiction.

Moreover, any reorientation of patterns of production and exchange towards BHN and self-sufficiency will impose restraints on established patterns of bourgeois consumption.[26] 'Taste-transfer' remains ubiquitous on the continent despite declines in incomes, both personal and national: the multinationals have been all too successful in creating demands for Western gadgetry as the rash of stereos in the 1970s and video recorders in the 1980s, let alone tinned baby milk since the 1960s, attests. Interestingly, few of the traits of Western 'alternative cultures' have been picked up by the African middle classes, other than perhaps jeans among self-consciously radical intellectuals (amongst whom are the originators of elements of the Monrovia strategy of self-reliance): the indigenous bourgeoisie remains more wedded to conspicuous consumption than its counterparts in the West. If import-substitution is to be succeeded by more self-sustaining production based on BHN rather than élite demands then the latter's lifestyles will have to change. Such indulgent lifestyles are, of course, under great pressure in the periphery in any case as inflation, unemployment, infrastructural decay and foreign-exchange crunches undermine established post-independence expectations and patterns.

TABLE 3·9 *African population factors compared to other regions*

Region	*Population growth (%) 1970–80*	*Urban population growth (%) 1970–80*	*Child death rate 1–4 years (%) 1979*	*Life expectancy at birth (years) 1979*	*Labour force (%) in (a) agriculture*	*(b) industry*
Africa sub-Sahara	2.8	5.5	22.3	47.0	77.6	8.1
Middle East and North Africa	2.8	4.6	15.5	54.0	42.6	24.2
East Asia and Pacific	1.5	2.9	4.5	60.8	50.5	16.4
South Asia	2.5	4.1	19.2	49.1	66.3	9.6
Latin America and Caribbean	2.6	3.9	6.6	63.6	30.2	23.7

SOURCE UNDP, *TCDC News,* 1982 (2), 2.
NB The dramatic caption to this table in a UN publication: 'According to statistics from UN organizations presented to the Libreville Conference, Africa sub-Sahara, compared to other developing regions, has the highest rates of over-all and urban population growth, the highest child death rate, the lowest life expectancy, the highest share of its population working in agriculture and the lowest in industry.'

As the African middle classes become marginalised so they are compelled to practise farming, moonlighting and/or 'smuggling' to survive along the lines of the 'black', informal economy in OECD states: indigenous professionals concentrate less and less on their formal roles and they chase food, petrol and spare parts. The alternative of self-reliance is, then, a prospect of planned rather than unplanned change; and as anarchy and starvation come closer so structural or 'willed' change, with at least the possibility of renewed development, may become more attractive with its roots in a continuing population explosion (see Tables 3·9 and 3·10). The very crisis of the continent may predispose otherwise antagonistic bourgeois (and proletarian) elements towards a reluctant acceptance of more internally oriented production. To this extent, the *Lagos Plan of Action* was indeed a timely statement.

When the continental *Plan* was discussed and drafted in the late-1970s by (more informed and enlightened) African intellectuals and decision-makers, it was conceived as (i) a response at the level of economics to the cyclical downturn of the second half of the 1970s, and (ii) a reaction at the level of politics or concepts to the unsatisfactory state of development achievements and assumptions. As a pragmatic tactical response at the level of policy and as a principled strategic reaction at the level of theory the *Lagos Plan* represented a considerable advance in pan-African thought. Although the prospects for political integration – a union or federation of states – or for strategic co-operation – a pan-African High Command or Security Council – have receded since independence, the possibilities of an economic community seem to have improved, in part because of the negative rates of growth experienced since the mid-1970s.

But pan-African economic nationalism is more than a collective statement of continental economic policy and more than a reaction to *dependencia* logic; it represents the first continental consensus on development direction in the mid-term future, with myriad implications for regional negotiations, national plans and class relations. Although, as already suggested, some regimes and interests may more than others identify with it *in toto* or in part, it now exists as an *indigenous* marker or check-list against which national priorities and performances can be evaluated. For, unlike the series of global statements, from the Pearson to the Brandt Commissions and unlike the competitive *Agenda for Action,* the *Lagos Plan* is an indigenous statement of collective experiences, expectations and prescriptions. The *Plan* represents, then, a considered response to (i) the disappointment of independence, (ii) the limitations of orthodox theory and policy, and (iii) the constraints of dependence.

Given the structural rather than cyclical crisis now confronting Africa and the world, it may also now be treated as a reaction to the post-neo-colonial and post-OPEC order, one in which self-reliance

TABLE 3·10 *Historic trends and normative scenario for Africa's demographic situation 1980 and 2008*

Demographic indicators	*Historic trends (high variant scenario)*			*'Willed future' (normative scenario)*		
	1980	*2008*	*Annual growth rate*	*1980*	*2008*	*Annual growth rate*
Total population	440	1077	3.2	439	997	2.9
Urban population	120	472	4.9	120	464	4.8
Rural population	320	605	2.3	319	533	1.8
Population aged 0–14	199	479	3.1	198	415	2.6
Population aged 15–64	228	564	3.2	228	550	3.1
Population aged 65+	13	34	3.4	13	32	3.2
Population aged 6–11 (primary education)	80	178	2.9	73	160	2.8
Population aged 12–17 (secondary education)	65	152	3.0	59	139	3.1
Population aged 18–23 (higher education)	58	124	2.7	48	120	3.3
Life expectancy at birth – males	50.1	60.5		50.1	58.2	
Life expectancy at birth – females	53.4	64.1		53.1	61.7	
Average completed family size	5.1	4.8		5.1	4.6	
Dependency ratio	94	91		94	82	
Net migration	22	0		22	0	

SOURCE ECA. *ECA and Africa's Development 1983–2008*, 22 and 58.

and self-sustainment may be inevitables rather than desirable options. Any progress in the implementation of the *Plan* and in the creation of an African Economic Community[27] before the end of the present century will affect not only country growth levels but also class inter-relations. Africa's place in the international division of labour has changed since independence despite the failures and frustrations of negotiations for an NIEO; the *Lagos Plan* reflects, and responds to, the continent's present and projected marginalisation in the post-Bretton Woods order.

Northern *paternalism,* in the shape of the Brandt Commission reports[28] and World Bank *Agenda,* has been repudiated along with Northern *protectionism:* 'mutuality' hardly exists between such divergent political economies whose position in the global economy is essentially antagonistic rather than compatible.[29] If the growing divergence is clear in structural terms it is increasingly apparent in pragmatic terms too; for not only is the North protectionist, it is also isolationist in mood, less prepared to provide aid, other than military, and finance, except to a few 'promising' or 'responsible' semi-peripheral regimes. In other words, it is becoming quite rational, as well as logical and ethical, for African states to support the *Lagos Plan;* there is, in truth, little alternative. The reformism of the *Plan* – incremental rather than haphazard change – stands in contrast to the two other conceivable futures other than static osmosis: repression or revolution.

REFORM, REPRESSION OR REVOLUTION?

If the *Lagos Plan* and its national adjuncts represent essentially pragmatic reformist responses to interrelated continental and global crises, then the alternatives to it in a situation of recession and regression are essentially twofold: anarchy or revolution. In the African context, the former consists largely of a return to local self-reliance in which the countryside looks after itself and declines to satisfy demands from the cities, while the latter involves popular challenges to incumbent regimes from within the proletariat, peasantry, party or military. Given the unattractiveness and uncertainness of either of these scenarios for established ruling classes, a degree of reform, however unacceptable in principle, may nevertheless be preferable.

The *Lagos Plan,* as suggested perhaps by its formal acceptance among the community of African presidents or ruling classes, has a certain anti-revolutionary as well as anti-conservative content. It is, in many ways, a consensual, nationalist reaction not only to alternative external pressures and proposals but also to active internal demands and dialectics: a collective form of 'defensive radicalism'[30] emanating from an enlightened element within the African intellectual fraction.

Such criticism is not intended to demean the instigators of, or detract from the intentions of, the *Plan.* Rather, it is to recognise that established African regimes were unlikely to be converted even to the marginal redefinition of development implied by the *Plan* unless under pressure. And the crisis-cum-conjuncture of the mid-1970s onwards posed sufficient challenge internally – for example, what to do with the growing ranks of unemployed and underemployed in a period of inflation, recession, debt and minimal foreign exchange – as well as externally – the NIEO debate juxtaposed with the reality of a new, no more attractive, international division of labour – for otherwise complacent and indulgent regimes to re-evaluate development directions and difficulties. Yet in addition to such relatively enlightened responses many ruling classes also espoused contrary schemes: they insisted on NIEO, demanded more assistance, pleaded for more attention and, most importantly, tightened their grip on power. In short, in the dialectic of treating the new conjuncture, different fractions espoused alternative solutions: reform *and* repression, inward-looking *and* outward-looking opportunities, counter-dependence *and* interdependence, and relevant as well as inappropriate technologies. Political exclusion co-existed with economic reform, strategic concentration with social change.

Nevertheless, it is important not to underestimate the relevance and resilience of the OAU strategy. For even if it is treated more by neglect than by implementation, at least it offers a counterpoise to either the continuation of inappropriate policies or the articulation of more conservative reactions: the privatisation of the World Bank or the monetarism of the IMF. The 'self-reliance' of the *Lagos Plan* stands, then, as a recognised and legitimised alternative to the 'conditionality' of *Agenda* and so affords support for more enlightened elements within national, regional and continental political economies. It remains for the originators and defenders of the *Plan* to assemble an effective 'transnational' coalition throughout the continent to advocate and implement its strategy; hence the importance of attempts by the ECA, OAU and others to mobilise political as well as economic support for effecting the *Plan*'s provisions in the variety of political economies found on the continent. Ironically, then, although the policy has counter-revolutionary overtones it is also subversive of some established values and regimes: the contradictions of reformism. In such an environment, the ECA may become *sub judice* in certain member states. As Adedeji recognises in his critique of mismanagement, wastage, 'leakage' and corruption on the continent and in his espousal of self-reliance and self-sustainment:

> A government without a vision and the will to translate such a vision into realities is a self-serving cabal. It is certainly not a government of the people for the people. Nor is it a government worthy of a developing country urgently in need of structural transformation.[31]

If the ECA Executive Secretary was a political scientist without diplomatic immunity in certain African societies he would be in some jeopardy, as noted in the conclusion on the risks of liberalism, let alone radicalism, on the continent today.

4 Prescription: What Is To Be Done?

'So long as incorporation into the world market/world division of labour is seen automatically to breed underdevelopment, the logical antidote to capitalist underdevelopment is not socialism, but autarky . . . the notion of the "development of underdevelopment" opens the way to third-worldist ideology.'—Robert Brenner, 'The Origins of Capitalist Development: A Critique of neo-Smithian Marxism', *New Left Review*, 104, July–August 1977.

'New departures, new experiments, new achievements combined to induce a sturdy scepticism about any kind of foreign model that might be recommended. There came the development of programmes for constructive change aimed at building indigenous models.'—Basil Davidson, *Africa in Modern History: the search for a new society* (Harmondsworth: Pelican, 1978) p. 376.

'. . . third historic possibility which lies before Africa is a march to fascism. This could come about in a situation where there was protracted economic stagnation but not yet revolution . . . one thing that would surely be needed in ever-increasing quantities in this situation would be repression . . . It would appear that the choice for Africa is not between capitalism and socialism after all, but between socialism and barbarism. Which will it be?'—Claude Ake, *Revolutionary Pressures in Africa* (London: Zed, 1978) p. 67.

The unhelpful inheritance, disappointing performance and unpromising prospects characteristic of the continent pose major problems for both politics and policy. As the Third UN Development Decade has dawned, African leaders both individually and collectively have begun to confront the challenges to the accumulative potential of their own positions and to the BHN of their populations. If, on the one hand, they fail to act decisively, global 'market forces' or international financial institutions such as the IMF and IBRD will make and effect decisions instead. On the other hand, daily preoccupations of personal and political survival make it difficult for them to identify, let alone treat, fundamental problems.

It is not coincidental, then, that the beginning of the eighties was marked by a major debate at the continental level between those in favour of disengagement and those still espousing incorporation: the *Lagos Plan of Action* and the *Agenda for Action*, respectively.[1] The April 1980 Lagos economic summit represented something of a watershed: Africans now want and are determined to design their own developmental strategies. They are also prepared to try a combination of old and new remedies such as ECOWAS, SADCC and the Eastern and Southern African Preferential Trade Area (PTA).

TOWARDS DEPENDENCE OR SELF-RELIANCE?

The *Lagos Plan* and the World Bank *Agenda* constitute divergent strategies at the continental level – self-reliance and renewed incorporation, respectively. The only other major variant would be some form of collective socialism; notwithstanding the number of self-proclaimed 'socialist' regimes in Africa this strategy has yet to be seriously advocated or discussed at the continental, or even regional, level. Self-reliance itself was not really considered or debated until the 1970s because the 1960s were years of economic expansion and political naïvety. As Basil Davidson suggests,

> The kind of thinking that emerged in the 1960s was not yet capable in a systematic way of questioning the accepted structures of the nation-state in Africa, nor was there, at least until after 1965, any sufficiently pressing reason for doing so; that would be the task of the 1970s.[2]

Africa displayed an aura of unity in its first decade of independence as most constituent territories merely went along with inherited institutions without attempting dramatic transformations, in part because economic difficulties were not yet pressing: the gap between political and economic power was not too gaping. As Philippe Lemaitre comments:

> [The] years 1960–1975 were ones of surprisingly homogeneous political arrangements in Africa. Most governments have been, relatively speaking, *status quo* oriented . . . the forms and modes of class conflict have been muted and repressed. Behind surface instability lay political continuity, that of a series of governments effectively controlled by middle classes using this control to advance themselves economically. If many of these national middle classes were doing only fairly well at best by international measurements, they were doing very well indeed by internal national measurements.[3]

However, post-1975 shocks eroded development prospects not only nationally but also for indigenous bourgeois classes, leading to dramatic innovations in economic strategy. Davidson has characterised this post-colonial period well:

> [The] working out of confrontation between the colonial heritage and the pre-colonial heritage, now that the second is free to challenge the first; and along with that, the resultant development of ideas concerned with searching for a different model. These are the fields of theory and practice within which this history plays out its ongoing and decisive themes into the 1980s and beyond.[4]

The most striking change to follow the demise of the Bretton Woods system is the appearance of several self-proclaimed 'Marxist–Leninist' regimes: up to 25 per cent of Africa's states claim to be Marxist, although the group is quite diverse – Angola and Mozambique, Benin and Congo, Ethiopia and Zimbabwe. But this 'socialist' strategy is one of four major variants which can be distinguished in contemporary Africa; the other three are state socialist, state capitalist and capitalist.

VARIETIES OF POLITICAL ECONOMY IN AFRICA

The majority of regimes remain 'state capitalist' or 'state socialist'; in these two types, as in the socialist category as well, the state apparatus is a dominant feature of both ideology and implementation. The fourth variety is distinctive because the state has a minimal role in it; but this straightforward 'capitalist' system has not been widely adopted in Africa. Instead, most analysts recognise a tripartite distinction among current development strategies on the continent: state capitalist, state socialist and socialist. Aguibou Yansané, for example, has pointed to three post-independence tendencies:

> First, the pragmatist reformist trend did not necessarily break the continuity of the colonial exchange and trade relations. Second, the noncapitalist approach . . . experienced many problems when attempts were made to set the economy and society in transition to scientific socialism. Third, other African colonies, which saw the need for an armed struggle to achieve independence, chose the revolutionary trend.[5]

Likewise, Davidson has proposed a trilateral categorisation given historical developments up to *circa* 1970:

> A first category now consisted of a few regimes with relatively strong economies. Their ruling groups could still add wealth and status to themselves, and, by continuing to grow, hope to become a middle class capable of building an indigenous capitalism.
>
> A second category was numerous. These were regimes with relatively weak economies in most or all of which the parliamentary model had decayed into an autocracy, but where, because of economic weakness, ruling groups had no thought of being able to grow into dominant middle classes. Often relying on foreign partners for their survival, these were bureaucratic dictatorships of a peculiarly crude type.
>
> A third category, few in number, was also composed of regimes with weak economies . . . These were the regimes that had turned away from the given model and its decadent derivatives, and were ready to experiment with democratic politics.[6]

This tripartite typology remains relevant for the current period, yet the characteristics of these distinctive political economies – state capitalist, state socialist and socialist[7] – have become more extreme and divergent since the mid-1970s. First, those state capitalist systems which are also NICs – Ivory Coast, Kenya and Nigeria – have become more capitalist as the role of the state has been assumed increasingly by the national bourgeoisie. Second, state socialist regimes which have been subjected to immense external pressures, such as Somalia, Tanzania and Zambia, have become more statist than socialist. While, third, socialist regimes dealing with an unhelpful global economy – Algeria, Angola and Mozambique – have tended to become more *laissez-faire* rather than collectivist.

Each of these three cases has revealed a new realism and consciousness about external obstacles, obstacles which necessitated innovative ideas and plans. So Davidson sees a novel and positive trend emerging in the new decade reflective of past disappointments and frustrations:

> [The] development of programmes for constructive change aimed at building indigenous models; and some of these, in the perspective of the 1980s, were manifestly within an entirely new field of independent thought, having discarded the various simulacra of other people's systems along with the rest of the decorative verbiage of the 1960s.[8]

On the contrary, however, taking contemporary changes into account, Lemaitre argues along the lines presented in the previous chapter that only the minority of capitalist or state capitalist political economies will grow in the remainder of the twentieth century:

> [The] next 15 to 25 years present relatively positive opportunities for Africa's semi-industrialising countries but a bleak picture for the largely agricultural ones. The minority able to exploit such an opportunity include Algeria, Nigeria, Zaire, the politically special case of South Africa, possibly Egypt, perhaps Zambia and Morocco, one day (but only later in time?) Angola.[9]

Given exponential divergence on the continent, the choice may become increasingly twofold again, between 'national capitalism' on the one hand and 'national socialism' on the other. Given the starkness of the choice, it will not be made easily, although global pressures force the relatively rich towards national capitalism and the very poor towards national socialism, with rather profound implications for Africa's cohesion and direction. As Thomas Kanza notes:

> The African states are still undecided as to which economic system

> they should adopt, although such a choice is fundamental to national development, planning and economic expansion . . .
>
> [They] are increasingly finding themselves faced with an absolute choice: should they adopt the traditional capitalist method, which means, in effect, dependence on foreign capital and subordination of their own development to the special interests of monopoly capitalism? Or should they, on the contrary, take the socialist road and plan their development rationally, in the general interest of Africa and its people?[10]

Lemaitre likewise dichotomises Africa's choices in the post-industrial, post-expansion world economy:

> [The] essential option of African states seems to be between governments controlled by internal middle class groups openly allied to governments and corporations in the industrialised world, and the more 'socialist', more autonomous, and more self-consciously indigenous regimes.[11]

But in reality the choice may not be either so stark or so straightforward as (i) African political economies have come to include significant indigenous interests since independence which cannot easily be disregarded, and (ii) international interests, along with their local associates, retain substantial influence in Africa, particularly in the semi-periphery. Petras *et al.* have, therefore, related three types of development strategy to salient characteristics of political economies such as those found in Africa:

> The postindependence regime can choose among at least three strategies or types of class alliances for capital accumulation. In the first instance, it can join with imperial firms and regimes in intensifying surplus extraction from the labour force through a variety of postindependence working relationships outlined under the rubric of dependent neo-colonialism. An alternative strategy for the national regime involves extracting the surplus from the labour force and limiting or eliminating the share going to the imperial firms, thus concentrating it in the hands of the state and/or private national entrepreneurs. This approach, which can be referred to as nationalist developmentalism without redistribution,

> leads to a concentration of income at the top of the national class hierarchy. A third alternative is for the national regime to ally itself with the labouring population, extend the areas of national control (through nationalisation), reinvest the surplus of the national economy, or promote a redistribution of income within the national class structure.[12]

Finally, one further type of development prospect needs to be recognised although this one is hardly desired by itself: anarchy. In a period of minimal economic growth, high population growth and global recession and inflation national economies may decay, leading to various forms of anarchy and fascism. The trend towards anarchy is clear in a group of states across middle Africa. For reasons of both civil strife and economic decline the political economies of Chad, Ghana, Uganda and Zaire have considerable anarchic elements: conflict, recession and inflation have led to the virtual destruction of their national economies. Now the ruling class exerts control not over a viable national system but over an economy dependent on smuggled external trade and foreign exchange. Corruption – *kalabule* or *magendo* – becomes widespread and the peasants and workers tend to return to the rural areas and to subsistence agriculture merely to stay alive. National exchange and communication, let alone accumulation, become minimal: self-reliance produces essentially regional economies within states which are fairly autonomous from each other, a reversion towards pre-colonial patterns of existence and co-existence. BHN – defined by the people, not by the state – become the watchword of the rural areas and local appropriate technologies tend to revive and flourish. Meanwhile, the decline in cash crop production depresses the remnants of the national economy ever further: reconstruction is increasingly problematic. The peasantry reverts to a relatively 'uncaptured' state having been incorporated in colonial and post-colonial times.[13]

Economic decline of a somewhat less dramatic variety may result in a tendency towards authoritarianism and fascism, as Claude Ake's opening quote to this chapter indicates: the state attempts to compensate for inadequate and declining forms of compensation – real incomes and quality of services have fallen significantly in the majority of countries – by increased control or repression. Unhappily, Amin's Uganda may not be *sui generis* but rather a generalisable fascist response to underdevelopment at the periphery in the post-Bretton Woods era.[14]

Paradoxically, the contemporary concern for human rights and needs in Africa has arisen at a time when both are more endangered than ever.[15] Human rights, however defined, are under threat from arbitrary rulers and unequal exchange; basic freedoms and needs are no longer recognised, let alone met. Notwithstanding either the OAU's adoption of the Banjul Charter on Human and People's Rights in Africa[16] or the ILO's espousal of basic needs strategies for African and other states,[17] human dignity and longevity are not being secured. As the first, relatively benign and liberal, leadership generation yields under pressure of circumstance to successor generations, so human liberties and requirements are ignored. The state has become increasingly bureaucratic and exclusive since independence as access to it or control over it have become ever more visibly the path to prosperity. Given the centrality of state structures, their dismantling for reasons of international fiat or internal subversion is unlikely unless one or other fraction becomes dominant. If the latter eventuality arises the state may become more autonomous and less ubiquitous; hence the attractions of capitalism and socialism without the statist adjective. But such a clear-cut resolution of antagonisms is relatively unlikely in all except a few states – those at the semi-periphery on the one hand and those where long liberation struggles have taken place on the other hand. Elsewhere, contradictions centred on the overdeveloped state are likely to continue, so exacerbating the seemingly endless cycle of coups, uncertainties and anarchy: a decidedly unattractive scenario.

TOWARDS CAPITALISM OR SOCIALISM?

Anarchy and fascism are two rather extreme prospects for the mid-term future, the products of persistent economic decline. Two other variants of established state-centric political economies may also be expected to emerge: capitalism and socialism. In part, any withering of the state in Africa may be caused by external pressures, particularly from the IMF and IBRD, but also from aid donors and capital investors, who blame over-centralisation for some of Africa's difficulties. But it may also be the product of largely internal social pressures: from the burgeoning national bourgeoisie in state capitalist systems and from proletarian interests in state socialist systems, both of whom may become hegemonic and so able to oversee the dismantling of certain state structures. Fawzi Mansour has outlined the transition from state capitalism towards capitalism, a transition most likely to occur within the semi-periphery:

> Barring a course of auto-centred self-reliant development, one or the other of the following three variants of the peripheral formation is bound to exist in African countries: neo-colonial, liberal-capitalist and bureaucratic capitalist. Looking a little further into the future it seems that the neo-colonial variant is the one that will be quickest to disappear. The neo-colonial variant exists where a local bourgeoisie did not have a chance to develop . . . But . . . a local bourgeoisie is bound to appear . . . and to present itself more and more insistently as a partner and/or a substitute for foreign capital, thus gradually transforming the regime into dependent liberal capitalism.[18]

The transition from state socialism towards socialism is somewhat more problematic given the essentially 'statist' origins of 'socialism' in much of the continent. In those situations where protracted guerrilla struggle occurred – Angola, Mozambique and Zimbabwe – or where anti-feudal 'revolution' took place – Ethiopia – the transitional 'state socialism' stage may be bypassed, although a retreat to it is always possible. Elsewhere, progress beyond state socialism is very difficult because, as Nicola Swainson indicates, '*Socialism* emerges as a *policy alternative* for the national bourgeoisie rather than being a product of class struggle.'[19] Unless proletarian and peasant forces are both insistent and respected, state socialist systems can just as easily move towards state capitalism as towards socialism, although social contradictions may thereby multiply and intensify. As Roxborough notes about socialism at the periphery:

> The socialism which exists in many countries of the Third World is indeed a lumpensocialism. What exists is a form of class rule in which the historical task of capital accumulation (abdicated by the bourgeoisie) is performed by a bureaucratic elite drawn from diverse petty bourgeois sectors. This elite retains state power through the most varied forms of corruption, nepotism and repression while it attempts to consolidate itself into a new capitalist class.[20]

But in a period of economic contraction, any consolidation by the bureaucratic bourgeoisie means further impoverishment for other social groups. To contain such social opposition necessitates increased repression, which is hard to sustain over time in an underdeveloped system. In short, contradictions of an 'over-developed' state in an 'under-developed' situation may lead to its own demise, so giving rise to a re-definition of, and renewed interest in, 'security' in Africa.[21] Although a series of 'petty-bourgeois' regimes may circulate in quick succession, eventually extra-bourgeois interests will intervene opening up wider prospects. As Samir Amin notes: '[The] deadlock . . . will . . . continue . . . until new social forces appear . . . capable of conceiving a strategy for liberation that goes beyond the narrow horizons of minor ex-colonial civil servants.'[22]

The appearance and persistence of more proletarian forces are by no means guaranteed, however. For although the state machinery in Africa is everywhere underdeveloped and usually inefficient – less so in, say, Banda's Malawi or Ahidjo's Cameroon than in Diouf's Senegal or Shagari's Nigeria – it retains considerable residual strengths, particularly if it can separate unionists from students, traders from peasants and professionals from the media; that is, if it can undermine or destroy promising anti-regime coalitions.[23] It remains symptomatic of regime resilience or repression that few major political changes occur on the continent other than through military coups or presidential decease. And even the surprisingly lengthy transition back to civilian from military rule in Nigeria no longer remains an exception to the rule.

The ability of regimes to remain in power even under pressure is not only a function of their resources, political or economic. Rather, it often reflects the external connections of the bourgeoisies in general and the leaders in particular, especially those situated in the semi-periphery. The bourgeoisies, particularly their comprador parts, retain strong transnational links with the international capital – banks, companies, aid agencies, communicators, etc. – while the leaders, especially their military components, retain strong transnational links with the international polity – governments, armies, intelligence agencies, international organisations, etc. Such connections provide escape and support in the good periods – state visits, aid projects, global conferences and current information – and, perhaps even more importantly, military *matériel*, debt relief, strategic intervention and political legitimation in the bad times. Normally, by definition and position, the proletariat and peasantry lack this type of external assistance. To be sure, international trade union, co-operative and guerrilla activities may rectify the balance somewhat, but such support is only salient in particular periods, usually when internal contradictions have already become quite antagonistic. By contrast, the ruling class retains its external support at all times; only its size, salience and character vary, depending on the internal situation and external conditions.

One of the scary things for the African bourgeoisie at the present time of global contraction is the possibility that in a post-neo-colonial period such regular transnational interest and support will evaporate, leaving it much more dependent on its own, declining resources. Certainly in a period of recession, external interests are becoming more selective and calculating, concentrating aid, investment and bases in the few 'promising' states at the semi-periphery rather than spreading decreasing resources evenly throughout the continent's periphery.

At the same time as external powers are becoming more calculating – resorting to military involvement when the chips are down because non-military support has been withdrawn or reduced – internal pressures are mounting in response to declining standards of living.[24] So the present crisis represents a peculiar opportunity to non-bourgeois forces both to increase their support among alienated and impoverished workers and farmers and to strike against decaying, disillusioned and isolated regimes.

It is into such a perplexing and problematic situation that the World Bank intrudes, attempting to revive external support for, and the internal strength of, African governments. Indeed, in a period of protectionist impulses in the North, 'internationalist' pressures of transnational corporations and global agencies may seek and serve to revive neo-colonial links (see concluding chapter). Yet in an essentially post-neo-colonial world such a perpetuation is quite problematic as Northern governments are rather calculating and African regimes are quite desperate. As Christine Bogdanowicz-Bindert argues in a recent lament for the 'unrealistic' set of projections and proposals to emanate from the World Bank, increased aid, investment, trade and commodity prices are all unlikely given Northern attitudes. Therefore she calls for attention to be paid to the 'unthinkable' – 'a situation in which there will be little or no progress in the region'.[25]

> [The] most fundamental assumptions underlying a significant improvement in sub-Saharan economic prospects are unrealistic.

The implication is for a continuation of economic stagnation and human misery, recurrent crises and stop gap measures.[26]

Whilst a few leaders and states – especially those at the semi-periphery – may receive the assistance, financial and material, which they seek the majority will not do so despite the World Bank's pleas to its internationalist coalition to be more generous and less mercantilist in hard times. This will leave most political economies at the mercy of 'market forces' externally – that is, decreasing terms of trade, high prices for loans and imported inflation – and 'radical' forces internally – underpaid and underemployed workers, impoverished peasants and a marginalised petty-bourgeoisie.

However, the continued ability of the African bourgeoisie to consume and accumulate despite inauspicious times and trends should not be excluded entirely, for through repressive state instruments they may yet be able to maintain their own personal lifestyles and savings even though the majority of their populations are unable to do so: authoritarian bourgeois rule encouraged or sanctioned by external interests may yet contain proletarian pressures at least in the crucial semi-periphery. Moreover, the 'African revolution' has been 'betrayed' so many times by successive leaders that the prospects for really radical change continue to recede. The conclusion puts such a pessimistic scenario into global perspective. But before turning to it, the major indigenous response to intense extracontinental constraints and intracontinental contradictions is examined: the 1980 *Lagos Plan of Action for the Economic Development of Africa, 1980–2000.*[27]

THE DIPLOMACY OF DEVELOPMENT: IBRD *v.* OAU

The *Lagos Plan of Action* is both ideology and strategy; a collective continental response to the global recession of the 1970s and to consequent African declines and crises. It is also a reaction to (i) the demise of development doctrine and performance since independence, and (ii) the projection of unattractive trends and scenarios for the two remaining decades of the twentieth century. Despite considerable differences in position and perception, polemic and potential the leaders of Africa together accepted the direction of the earlier 1979 Monrovia Symposium and adopted the concept of self-reliance as the motif for the continent in the difficult days of a post-Bretton Woods, post-expansionist system. They did so not because they had all become converts to a 'small is beautiful' ethic Rather, in a competitive and contracting global economy they had little choice. While a few states might continue to grow for particular reasons, the majority are likely to be at best stagnant and at worst in decline until the year 2000.[28] To accumulate, African leaders, like leaders everywhere, need to remain in power. The *Lagos Plan of Action* constitutes a life-saving strategy to turn adversity into advantage and isolation into an adventure. In short, it represents a collective attempt to revive, in the context of economic recession, the populist coalition which characterised the stage of political nationalism in the 1950s. This consensual declaration of economic nationalism – disengagement and reorientation – is a response by hegemonic interests to the imperatives of the 1980s: external disinterest, economic difficulty, domestic alienation and problematic projections.[29] It represents a distinctive combination of *dependencia* logic, relevant policies and anticipated antagonisms: a form of 'defensive radicalism'[30] on a continental scale. These several strands – developmental, intellectual, ideological, and individual – are well reflected in the words of a leading advocate and activist on African self-reliance, Adebayo Adedeji, the Executive Secretary of the ECA:

> [The] African economy today is the most open and the most exposed economy in the world, overly dependent on external trade and other external stimuli, foreign technology, and foreign expertise. The very strategies of development the African governments have been pursuing since independence have come from the outside, derived as they were from theories of economic development that were developed during the colonial pattern of production in Africa . . . The cumulative result is that, today, neither high rates of growth or diversification, nor an increasing measure of self-reliance and self-sustainment has been achieved in the African economy.[31]

To escape from inherited dependence and to avoid the pressures of decline, as well as to transcend predicted marginalisation and immiseration, African leaders momentarily overcame their ideological and political differences to agree on the creation of a continental economic community by the year 2000: a nice inheritance bequeathed to future generations of rulers. Given the intensity of the contemporary crisis – can it be transformed into a conjuncture?[32] – characterised by 'inter-imperial rivalries' and inter-African recession, they decided to seize the opportunity to abandon past policies and to avoid projected problems. As Adedeji warns, the 1980s are crucial as either turning point or further decay:

> For Africa, the 1980s – the United Nations Third Development Decade – will be particularly critical. Unless the fundamental strategic changes I have advocated and the alternative policies that flow from such changes are introduced and become effective during the decade, the chances of installing a new national economic order in African countries and a new regional economic order in Africa as a whole – based on an increasing measure of national and collective self-reliance and self-sustained growth – will be permanently aborted.[33]

Awareness of the incidences and implications of this unattractive *African Condition*[34] spread slowly in the second half of the seventies but as the recession intensified with cumulative results so the imperative of (re)action increased.

Characteristic of Africa's predicament, though, it has not been allowed to design and direct its own strategy undiverted: the World Bank has also produced a proclaimed diagnosis and cure for the condition. Unlike the collective class action and economic nationalist tone of the Lagos Plan, *Agenda for Action*[35] attempts to blame Africa for its own plight and to increase rather than reduce external incorporation and orientation. The two prescriptions represent divergent assumptions and interests; they stand in a dialectical relationship towards each other, as recognised in a combined OAU, ECA and ADB response: 'It is quite clear that the total effect of the [World Bank] recommendations addressed to African governments could very well make Africa more dependent and less self-reliant.'[36]

Although the two reports do agree about the seriousness of the crisis confronting Africa – inflation, recession, debt, import dependence, infrastructural decay, etc. – they disagree quite fundamentally on both causes of, and remedies for, this condition. The World Bank's criticism of internal factors and its advocacy of external orientation represents the revival and revision of 'modernisation' perspective as outlined in Chapter 1; by contrast the OAU focus on external factors and its espousal of inward-oriented development constitutes the acceptance of *dependencia* assumptions. The route to escape for the Bank – more external exchange and international assistance – is, for the OAU, the cause of present and projected difficulties. While the latter seeks 'rapid self-reliance and self-sustaining development',[37] in part through state intervention and substantial industrialisation, the former still prefers a 'growth-oriented programme: (i) more suitable trade and exchange-rate policies; (ii) increased efficiency of resource use in the public sector; and (iii) improvement in agricultural policies.'[38]

The OAU reaction to the continental crisis involves, on the one hand, a denial of growing inequalities among as well as within African states and, on the other hand, an attempt to turn protectionist and isolationist pressures in the North to good advantage: to transform crisis into conjuncture by putting 'Africa first' instead of allowing it to be further marginalised: 'self-reliance . . . is not to say that the continent should totally cut itself off from outside contributions. However, these outside contributions should only supplement our own effort; they should not be the mainstay of our development.'[39] By contrast, the IBRD response, by excluding North and South Africa, emphasises differences and denies protectionist and isolationist impulses inside the OECD states; and it advances 'internationalist' linkages despite their uneven results in the past and their uncertain constituencies in the present (see next chapter). The *Agenda* advocates a return to the soil – to the further expansion of commodity exports – whereas the *Plan* continues to prefer industry as a means to minimise both dependence and vulnerability.

So the OAU sees disengagement as the prerequisite for development whereas the Bank still argues that 'trickle-down' will eventually generate growth notwithstanding the minimal rates of expansion of Northern economies in recent years. Ironically, then, the former blames external conditions and advances an internal solution – a continental common market – whereas the latter situates the causes of underdevelopment internally – inappropriate policies and processes – yet advocates an external solution. Moreover, the Bank is concerned with individual African states and with exchange rather than production, whereas the OAU deals with the collectivity of member states and with production, not just trade.

In spite of all the evidence of dramatic drops in both the terms of trade and foreign capital inflows, the Bank still offers a simplistic and paternalistic explanation for Africa's negative balances of trade and growth: 'external forces were not the chief factor behind growing deficits: for the oil-importing African nations as a group, poor export performance was more significant.'[40] The OAU coalition rejects such outmoded analysis and in response has sharpened its own perspective, arguing that acceptance of *Agenda* will merely perpetuate Africa's dependence on external values and factors:

> We are . . . concerned about the general tone of the [IBRD] report which tends to suggest that the region's problems are entirely of its own making and that unless the outsiders are allowed to come in with aid and new policies, the crisis would get out of hand and the result will be catastrophic.[41]

However, while the African coalition insists on self-reliance through public sector industrialisation, and its declaration represents a turning point in the OAU's collective foreign policy involving the redefinition of pan-Africanism in terms of economic liberation and unity, there remain ambiguities in its stance. The ideology of self-reliance is more acceptable to some interests on the continent than to others.

If the typology of political economies presented earlier in this chapter has any validity then reactions to the alternatives and competitive reports might vary accordingly. Given the more interventive and socialist inclinations of state socialist and socialist regimes they might be expected to be most supportive of the statist, self-reliant and industrial priorities of the *Lagos Plan of Action.* By contrast, the rather *laissez-faire* and capitalist inclinations of state capitalist and capitalist systems give them a positive predisposition towards the voluntaristic, extroverted and agricultural preferences of *Accelerated Development in sub-Saharan Africa.* To be sure, as indicated in the next chapter, ministries, parastatals and classes within such political economies may advocate contrary values; but hegemonic interests as represented in dominant coalitions will tend to identify with compatible forms of ideology and strategy.

Self-reliance has already been declared as a national strategy among a set of more radical and peripheral, 'socialist' states – Angola, Benin, Congo (B), Ethiopia and Tanzania, for example – while some state socialist and state capitalist regimes remain ideologically and structurally ambivalent – e.g. Malawi, Senegal and Zambia. The minority of more overtly capitalist states at the semi-periphery – Egypt, Ivory Coast, Kenya and Nigeria, for instance – may still hope to benefit from continued, even intensified incorporation in the world system despite recession and protectionism in the North; while still others – those in the anarchistic group – have in many ways lost whatever they had of a national economy – Chad, Gambia, Ghana, Sudan and Uganda – because of a combination of black market, smuggling and foreign-exchange 'leakages'. Indeed, the withdrawal of commodities, including labour, from these national economies and the return of self-sufficient subsistence existence – with all sorts of revived and 'relevant' technologies – constitutes a dramatic, if uncoordinated, form of intra-national self-reliance, not one which most African regimes, let alone the OAU, would want to encourage.

If the more radical and peripheral governments can identify most readily with the *Lagos Plan* then the less radical, semi-peripheral countries may do so least. Notwithstanding the pressures for an African consensus, the latter retain some confidence in orthodox developmentalist approaches because they have experienced relatively rapid growth rates themselves thus far. So those at the semi-periphery serve not only as markets for OECD capital and technological exports but also as examples of 'successful' orthodox growth policies: the 'models' which *Agenda* wants other less advantaged African states to emulate, as if all can expand simultaneously.

So, in general, the more capitalist, semi-peripheral political economies are least supportive of the OAU strategy and most comfortable with the IBRD prescription. They will go along at the collective diplomatic level with the *Lagos Plan of Action,* and as 'cores' at the semi-periphery they may even benefit from a continental common market, yet national negotiations will encourage redefinitions of incorporation rather than disengagement. And given the new uncertainties of import-substitution and export-based industrialisation in Africa,[42] they will keep their options open, as well as their credibility secure, by accepting certain advantages from the *Lagos Plan of Action* as regional centres. Nevertheless, the major actors in the African coalition are the Fourth World regimes of the real periphery. The latter are most threatened by international recession and protection; and they are most fearful of following Ghana and Uganda into an anarchic state. In response to such dilemmas of underdevelopment, many regimes have begun to adopt a type of strategy applied to Latin America to reduce popular demands and to achieve the conditions for growth: corporatism.

TOWARDS ANARCHY OR CORPORATISM?

Despite their profound differences, the *Plan* and *Agenda* both seek to improve Africa's unpromising developmental prospects. To this extent they each reflect the interests of the continent's ruling classes in generating sufficient surplus – sufficient for themselves and their states – for some accumulation to occur. Where such surplus is minimal and accumulation is insufficient, regimes may be tempted to adopt some variety of corporatism: an exclusive and structured political system. Where such surplus is absent and accumulation through production and taxation is impossible, as in the advanced decay of economies such as Ghana or Uganda, then plunder through coercion may be the only feasible tactic. The latter situation of anarchy represents the fate which the OAU and IBRD proposals seek to avoid for neither indigenous nor international interest can really benefit thereby, except through a very crude form of enrichment.[43] Because neither of these antithetical strategies are likely to be implemented in their entirety, though, many regimes are moving towards corporatist solutions as the means to maximise control over declining rates of surplus. Hegemonic forces may thereby protect their own interests; proletarian and peasant interests would be further excluded and repressed.

The imperative of corporatism,[44] in a global economy of minimal growth and national economies of marginal expansion, is a reflection of the increasing domestication of opposition and contradiction. Given the oversimplification of dependence perspectives, 'Third Worldist' ideology is misleading rhetoric: not all people stand to benefit from economic pan-Africanism. Indeed, there is considerable evidence that since independence the poor in Africa have become poorer while the rich have gradually accumulated more. This tendency towards inequality has intensified with the onset of recession and has profound implications for theory, policy and strategy. As Marcussen and Torp suggest:

> Where the dependency theorists saw the relations between centre and periphery as a situation of deadlock, in which the countries of the Third World were continuously being deprived of their economic surplus – a situation which they could only avoid by breaking with the world market – our study indicates that there seems to exist now a possibility for capital accumulation process within the context of capitalist development, at least in some

> countries of the periphery . . . These tendencies imply that the common interest of Third World workers, peasants and the bourgeoisie – so often postulated by the dependency theorists – in breaking with the world market remains a myth in a situation where the bourgeosie in the periphery is strengthening its material base to an ever increasing extent.
>
> This leads to the conclusion that, while the dependency theorists saw the dominant contradiction as being between developed and developing countries, the material changes in the world economy on the threshold of the 1980s are bringing about a situation where the internal class contradictions are becoming manifest in the centre as well as in the periphery – and, in the process, pushing aside the predominance of nationalist and populist ideology.[45]

The intensification of class contradictions at the periphery, directed against national as well as extranational bourgeois interests, has undermined African cohesion and direction. Hence the imperative of a new development strategy to overcome the impact of recession on the size and character of national political economies. But agreement on, let alone implementation of, this remains elusive precisely because of new diversities between as well as within the states of Africa, exacerbated by inter-imperial rivalries in the post-Bretton Woods global division of labour.[46] Meanwhile, although debates about *Plan* and *Agenda* and differentiations between semi-periphery and periphery proceed, corporatist impulses are widespread.

Corporatism comes in several guises depending on the character of political economy – the bureaucratic authoritarian and populist variants are most relevant in Africa[47] – but it is generally typified by rather structured and centralised tendencies. Unlike the inclusive and egalitarian nature of the political nationalist movement, the present period of economic nationalism is hardly populist, notwithstanding rhetoric to the contrary. The expansionist and optimistic period of the late 1950s and early 1960s produced rather open and large ruling coalitions; the contractions and pessimism of the late 1970s and early 1980s have encouraged closed and narrow coalitions which have confined many classes and fractions to either marginalisation or opposition. The corporatist urge is not exclusively military in content, although in some regimes the military are central. Rather it is a characteristic tendency to concentrate power, decision-making and property in a few hands.

Given Africa's low level of industrialisation and high level of dependence, as well as increasing degrees of inequality and antagonism, patterns of corporatism are defined largely by the state. It structures the whole political process into 'systems of interest representation based on non-competing groups that are officially sanctioned, subsidised and supervised by the state'.[48] So 'interest groups' in Africa are largely singular and circumscribed: one trade union, youth movement, women's association, even religious organisation, etc. per country.

The trend towards more exclusive forms of corporatism has been encouraged by the relentless recession of recent years. According to Alfred Stepan, 'inclusionary corporatism' is most likely in the early stages of import-substitution, a process which, in turn, is most common in periods of expansion. By contrast, 'exclusionary corporatism' is most likely to follow (as well as precede?) the import-substitution phase, as 'the pattern of industrial development begins to stagnate, the political economic struggle intensifies, and politics is increasingly seen in zero-sum terms'.[49] Although import-substitution has not proceeded far in many African states, in Kenya and the Ivory Coast it has done so. But their continued expansion is threatened by global recession;[50] recent disturbances there may lend support to Stepan's assertion and suggest an interrelationship between, on the one hand, import-substitution and global conditions and, on the other hand, between global conditions and patterns of corporatism.

In general then, in spite of variations among African political economies and regime ideologies, the growing involvement of the state in Africa has led, through various forms of corporatism, away from initial populist urges and towards more 'bureaucratic-authoritarian' regimes. If the former type is reflective of the optimism and expansionism of the post-war nationalist period then the latter is suggestive of a greater degree of pessimism and contraction of the post-Bretton Woods, post-independence era.

During the populist period, 'mass' politics and consumption were encouraged to advance both integration and growth. But as neither trickle-down nor take-off occurred, while the accumulative propensities of the new class remained strong, the contradiction between bourgeois wants and proletarian needs intensified. To advance their interests, the bureaucratic bourgeoisies began to extract more surplus in exchange for fewer services while advocating order over change.

Their particular bureaucratic–authoritarian form of corporatism has been well described by Guillermo O'Donnell for Africa as well as for Latin America:

> i) the exclusion of a previously politically activated popular sector; ii) the reconstitution of mechanisms of capital accumulation in favour of large public and private organisations; iii) the emergence of a new coalition whose principal members are state personnel (especially the military and civilian technocrats), international capital, and the segments of the local bourgeoisie which control the largest and most dynamic national business; and iv) the expansion of the state.[51]

It is this situation of centralisation and bureaucratisation which so exercises the World Bank; yet the condition is substructural and not superstructural, particularly in those few post-import-substitution situations where, exacerbated by external recession, relations have moved quite rapidly from mixed-sum to zero-sum. Class antagonisms have intensified because of the visibility of bourgeois consumption and the exclusion of non-bourgeois demands. The bureaucracy has become supreme and intolerant of popular participation and politicisation. Welfarist notions such as basic human needs are increasingly overlooked and opposed as 'socialist' and/or 'interventionist' ideas. Certain strands in the World Bank *Agenda* can be extracted to encourage the further expansion of this new class as it seeks to revive economies and eliminate subsidies.[52]

Finally, corporatism is not only a response to class interests, national decline and international difficulty. It is also a defensive reaction to the fear and incidence of anarchy as revealed by Bokassa and Nguema. Given the combination of external and internal pressures, African bourgeoisies, bureaucratic and otherwise, have relatively little room for manoeuvre; hence corporatism is a response to present problems and anticipated difficulties as well as the avoidance of decay and disorder. In the concluding chapter which follows, such 'choices' are considered as background to the revival and redefinition of 'security' and 'conflict' on the continent in the final two decades of the twentieth century.

Conclusion – Prospect: Constraints and Contradictions in a Post-Industrial World

'The study of political science would certainly gain considerably in realism and relevance by focusing attention on the *roots of politics* at the levels of production, social relations and social organisation of class forces. But political scientists may also contribute significantly to an understanding of *the impact of politics* on economic and social forces and the contradictions and struggles to which they give rise. At the level of theory, *both* concerns require an understanding of the dialectical relationship of determination and interaction which connect the economic and political levels of society.'—Bjorn Beckman, 'Political Science and Political Economy', in Yolamu Barongo (ed.) *Political Science in Africa: a critical review* (London: Zed, 1983) p. 110.

'[An] increasing measure of self-reliant and self-sustaining development and economic growth is a most important accompaniment of political independence since it would lead to the economic decolonisation of Africa.'

'Riots, crimes and misery would be the order of the day by the year 2008, if present trends were to continue. And with the weak and fragile socio-political systems, the sovereignty of African states, or whatever may still remain of it, will then be seriously at stake. Indeed . . . Africa marching toward the future hand in hand with the past and the present has no dignified future at all.'— Adebayo Adedeji, 'The Evolution of the Monrovia Strategy and the Lagos Plan of Action: A Regional Approach to Economic Decolonisation' (Addis Ababa: ECA, 1983) pp. 10 and 21.

'[Political] functions of the existing paradigms detract from the proper responsibility of political science. Even in its present

> fairly conservative form, political science, although very popular in Nigerian universities, has often been regarded as subversive to Nigeria's development process by both military and civil politicians, regime experts and functionaries, economic planners and bureaucrats. It is a discipline conceived as having unsettling effect on rulers, regimes and the political community.'— S. Egite Oyovbaire, 'The Tyranny of Borrowed Paradigms and the Responsibility of Political Science: The Nigerian Experience', in Yolamu Barongo (ed.) *Political Science in Africa: a critical review* (London: Zed, 1983) p. 247.

The analysis as well as the practice of political economy in Africa are in a state of flux as the continent moves beyond the midway point between independence in the early 1960s and the end of the twentieth century. The dialectics both between economics and politics, and between explanation and prescription, are at a crucial conjuncture as the continental crisis intensifies. Given the ongoing nature of these processes a fully fledged conclusion-cum-projection would be quite inappropriate, as well as open to the passage of time. Instead, this modest 'prospect' merely seeks to pull together some of the major questions, concepts and concerns raised already in the text, with the aspiration that this might clarify alternative modes of analysis and response.

IDEOLOGY AND REALITY: POLEMICS AND PROFESSIONALISM

There is, of course, a dialectical relationship between analysis and *praxis,* in both professional and political realms: what we perceive is affected by both mode of enquiry and type of reaction. Just as the modernisation school focused on superstructural relations and prescriptions – more institutionalisation would lead to development – so materialist scholars concentrate on substructural contradictions and syntheses – further antagonism will generate transformation. Both genres contain some elements of insight, but the latter is considerably more rich and powerful than the former. Yet the dialectic between substructure and superstructure can be no more one-sided in Africa than elsewhere: production is not the sole determinant of social relations, merely the primary one. Of course, political discourses and decisions, particularly in state-centric polities, affect the economy as well as vice versa; but the primary level and factor is economic. Yet neither economistic nor *dependentista* perspectives should be applied in a mechanistic or structuralist manner, as this overlooks nuance – what would Africa be without rumour and intrigue? – which can be crucial to explanation. Hence, as Beckman insists, the imperative of a subtle *neo*-Marxist approach, paying appropriate attention to 'developments at the level of production':

> This contrasts with the strong economic determinism usually postulated. Most crudely, 'neo-colonialism' . . . is taken to explain everything at the political level without any sustained effort to examine neo-colonialism itself and what it actually means at the level of the development of productive forces, social relations of production, class contradictions, and so on.
>
> Marxist political economy may lend itself to crudely deterministic application; still it is the only theoretical framework, as far as I know, which seriously and consistently addresses itself to . . . fundamental aspect(s) of social theory.[1]

If a neo-Marxist approach implies certain styles of policy prescription – popular control of production, production for welfare rather than accumulation, integrated national rather than global production, etc. – so it also suggests particular types of professional behaviour – attention to the roots of action, concern for labour as well as for capital, appreciation of contradiction and synthesis, etc. Not that all neo-Marxist scholars are radical or socialist in political orientation, although many tend to be so. Rather, a materialist perspective does impose certain basic standards of research and response.

En passant, then, one of the issues thereby raised by choice of approach is the professional–political one of the role of social, especially political, scientists in the development of the continent. Clearly, African (and Africanist) political scientists have begun to make a significant contribution to the development of the discipline, reorienting its 'developmental' perspective away from modernisation towards materialism.[2] This process is uneven both on and off the continent, yet the trend is incontrovertible and, hopefully, irreversible. Indeed, the trend has been established by both non-political scientists and non-academics. In particular, economists and other social scientists at and around the ECA have played a crucial role in popularising and legitimising more critical and creative, albeit non-Marxist, forms of enquiry and policy in Africa just as the Brandt Commission activities and reports have done at the global level. As Adedeji indicates in his survey of the sociology of the doctrine of self-reliance, since 1975–6 – the first period of energy and other economic shocks – the continental Commission has been

> seeking not merely an alternative strategy of development for Africa but also . . . a development strategy that is genuinely African-oriented, that is genuinely native rather than a strategy intended to lead to a caricature of the lifestyle of ways of living of one or the other of the existing socio-political systems or societies.[3]

This process of reconsidering approach, redefining development and reorienting strategy preceded the Monrovia consultation and Lagos summit by some four years: the ECA's *Revised Framework*[4] for implementing an NIEO in Africa which coincided with the first energy shocks and the mid-period of global negotiations to design a successor order to Bretton Woods. As Adedeji, with justifiable pride, recounts, the ECA has been in the vanguard of the interrelated intellectual and prescriptive redirection, in part because of unpromising scenarios based on then-emerging trends:

> The importance of ECA's *Revised Framework* is that it provided the main intellectual and theoretical foundation for the preparation of the Monrovia strategy and the Lagos Plan of Action, including the Final Act of Lagos. Its immediate impact arose from the challenge it posed to conventional wisdom in the field of development economics as it applies to the African realities . . . And its lasting contribution lay in its clear and precise definition of the meaning and scope of self-reliance in Africa.[5]

So this hitherto rather undistinguished, unimportant and unradical international organisation began, as the global and continental crisis intensified in the mid-1970s, to lay the foundation for an innovative approach at the level of theory and policy to Africa's political economy.[6] This served to reinforce an emerging intellectual trend, controversial though it was and is for some, towards political economy in general and materialism in particular.[7]

The place of the scholar in his/her home or host political economy – even if not in the ECA – is still more controversial, particularly when social scientists, like other intellectuals are becoming ever more marginal in most individual African states. So aside from the perplexing question of how exclusively 'professional' academics can be in a continent characterised by declining living standards, infrastructural quality and industrial performance, one issue remains the difficult personal-cum-political choice between survival and objectivity. Given the range of political economies found on the continent, the place and safety of the social critic obviously varies. Under the majority of exclusive regimes, individual security of tenure, if not life, is endangered when criticism is too sharp. Unhappily, this characteristic of intolerant administrations is found on both ends of the political spectrum – state socialist and state capitalist alike, as university closures and and pressures in Tanzania and Zambia, and in the Ivory Coast and Kenya, respectively illustrate. The place of the political scientist in overtly repressive regimes like those of Idi Amin or Kamuzu Banda is quite straightforward – immense discretion or considerable endangerment – which has led numerous colleagues into exile, opposition and, unhappily, their graves. The physical demise of Attati Mpakati of Malawi, or Ruth First[8] or Rick Turner of South Africa, or Herbert Chitepo of Zimbabwe are, sadly, no longer isolated cases. And in addition to the guerrilla leadership of people like Nathan Shamuyarira of Zimbabwe and Yoweri Museveni of Uganda, other brave colleagues have been imprisoned for their beliefs: Robert Molteno and Lionel Cliffe in Zambia, Ernest Wamba-dia-Wamba of Zaire *et al.*

Several others have been associated with a variety of progressive parties or regimes: Ibbo Mandaza in Zimbabwe, Emma Hansen in Ghana, Amos Sawyer in Liberia. But the role of social commentator let alone critic, is never a comfortable one, as Egite Oyovbaire's opening citation indicates; even 'pluralist' regimes sometimes have short fuses.

And if the place of indigenous analyst is tenuous, that of expatriate Africanist is even more so. Yet to eschew criticism is surely to be guilty of reverse paternalism or racism. One of the few positive functions of foreign radicals is not to be 'intellectual missionaries' but rather to be critical voices where indigenous scholars have to remain carefully mute: an advantage of residing in the metropole rather than the periphery. Similarly, we should counteract the unhelpful legacy of early modernisation 'pioneers' who left behind an inappropriate paradigm. Yet this should be discarded not because it is foreign but because it is wrong-headed.

Meanwhile, we might usefully bury the Mazrui-perpetuated diatribe and diversion about Marxism as another foreign ideology.[9] Materialism as mode of analysis is of universal applicability. To be sure, it needs to be modified to embrace contemporary, and historic, Africa. But to reject substructural contradictions simply because the mode was first employed in nineteenth-century Europe is to confuse or camouflage conservatism with nationalism. It is only possible to accept Oyovbaire's rhetorical plea if it applies to inappropriate styles as opposed to sources of analysis: 'political science must decolonise its own frameworks – must liberate itself from the tyrannies of import substitution.'[10] If the country or continental biases of political analysis are clear so too are their class affiliation: pan-Africanist scholars are as a whole no less bourgeois in origin and orientation than expatriate ones.

CLASS BASES OF POLITICAL ECONOMY AND FOREIGN POLICY

Essentially, the study of government means the study of the exercise of power and property by a particular ruling class. Likewise, the analysis of inter-state relations has typically meant the analysis of interactions among ruling classes. However, a more structural perspective recognises the internal and external limits on such classes given contradictions in production and distribution. Therefore, a neo-Marxist approach identifies the place of each fraction in the political economy and abstracts the underlying pattern of relations. The focus is on dialectic and antagonism rather than on compatibility and co-operation.

From this materialist perspective, development or foreign policy is merely the articulation of dominant class concerns rather than the expression of a transcended 'national interest'. Such an approach has only recently and infrequently been adopted to the analysis of African political economy and yet its insights are multiple and fruitful; and its potential for policy and planning considerable, even if still subject to considerable, often lively, discussion and interpretation.

We have already treated some of the central features of African contradictions and coalitions: the interaction between substructure and superstructure, the emergence of antagonistic fractions as well as classes, the divergent foreign connections of different elements

TABLE C·1 *Average annual rates of real growth in economic indicators, 1966–76 and 1981 (percentages)*

	Population		*Total GNP*		*Per capita GNP*		*Agricultural production*		*Manufacturing production*		*Gross investment*	
	1966–1976	*1981*	*1966–1976*	*1981*	*1966–1976*	*1981*	*1966–1976*	*1981*	*1966–1976*	*1981*	*1966–1976*	*1981*
Developing Countries	2.4	2.1	6.1	2.2	3.6	0.2	2.9	4.1	8.3	4.8	8.9	5.3
North Africa and Middle East	2.8	3.1	8.1	0.6	5.1	−2.5	2.4	−2.9	7.3	8.8	16.1	10.0
Africa	2.6	2.7	5.0	2.2	2.3	−0.5	1.6	3.6	7.1	8.4	10.9	−1.3
Latin America	2.6	2.3	5.9	−0.4	3.2	−2.6	2.9	4.8	7.0	3.4	7.8	−1.9
East Asia	2.4	1.6	8.1	5.5	5.5	3.8	3.8	4.7	15.6	5.8	12.3	6.3
South Asia	2.3	2.4	3.7	5.9	1.4	3.5	2.7	5.8	4.5	8.3	4.0	6.7
Europe	1.5	1.6	6.0	2.4	4.5	0.8	3.9	0.2	8.4	0.2	6.4	−0.2
Developed Countries	0.8	0.6	4.2	1.3	3.3	0.7	2.8	1.8	3.9	0.3	4.5	

SOURCE *US Foreign Policy and the Third World: Agenda 1983* (New York: Praeger for ODC, 1983) p. 225.

within peripheral social formations, the difference between cyclical and structural changes in global and local economies, the tension between mode of analysis and of prescription, the dialectic of reform, revolution and repression, and the alternative futures of further incorporation or increasing self-reliance. One common thread runs throughout these central contradictions: *increasing divergencies between and within the classes and countries of Africa exacerbated, of course, by their various historic and current linkages with external states, companies and institutions.*

In turn, these divergencies are inseparable from intensified competition and contradiction within the world system as a whole, particularly among the advanced industrialised states. As the 1983 *Economist* review of the world economy indicates, quoting Wellington at Waterloo: 'Hard pounding this, gentlemen, let's see who will pound longest.'[11] This pounding has shaken economies everywhere, but nowhere more so than in Africa. The exponential *marginalisation* of the continent by comparison to other regions has profound implications for the satisfaction of Basic Human Needs (see Tables C·1 and C·2) and is reflected in data on external exchange flows and balances (see Table C·3 and C·5). Although terms of trade capture only one element of the crisis, their divergence for different groups of African states is clear (see Table C·6) and will continue no matter what the price of oil. As the latest *World Development Report* recognises: 'The poorest developing countries – especially those in sub-Saharan Africa – have been the hardest hit by the current recession.'[12] And the Bank proceeded to warn of a continuation of such a crisis unless, from its modernisation perspective, appropriate domestic policies were adopted:

> The position of the low-income sub-Saharan African countries continued to deteriorate in 1980–82. Most had fared significantly worse in the 1970s than the 1960s, and GDP per capita declined in many countries from 1973 to 1980 . . . inappropriate policies – chronic fiscal deficits, farm prices and marketing arrangements that deterred production, and over-valued exchange rates – contributed to slow growth in the 1970s. These long-standing problems have been greatly exacerbated by the 1980–82 recession.[13]

By contrast, the ECA, reflective of the African consensus, seeks to turn such adversorial conditions into an advantage by abandoning

TABLE C·2 *Economic and social indicators, by region*

	Africa	*Asia*	*Latin America*	*Oceania*	*Europe*	*North America*	*OPEC*
Mid-1982 population (millions)	498.0	2622.2	377.0	23.1	806.3	256.4	353.8
Region's population as share of world population	10.9%	57.2%	8.2%	0.5%	17.6%	5.6%	7.7%
Average per capita GNP (1981)	$770	$973	$2044	$8593	$6595	$12 406	$1841
Average PQLI	43	62	75	87	90	96	52
Average birth rate (per 1000)	47	30	32	21	17	16	41
Average death rate (per 1000)	17	11	8	8	10	9	
Average life expectancy (years)	49	58	63	69	71	74	15
Average infant mortality rate (per 1000 live births)	120	79	64	27	29	12	103
Average literacy rate	36%	57%	79%	89%	95%	99%	50%
Average per capita education expenditures	$32	$41	$63	$398	$289	$680	$67
Average per capita military expenditures	$26	$40	$22	$162	$293	$508	$109

SOURCE *US Foreign Policy and the Third World: Agenda 1983* 224.

TABLE C·3 *Value of exports (billions of US dollars)*

	1960	*1970*	*1980*
Major oil-exporting countries	0.927	4.721	63.863
Non-oil-exporting countries	3.965	7.982	25.773
Developing Africa	4.892	12.703	89.636

SOURCE ECA, *Silver Jubilee Meetings,* April–May 1983, p. 27.

TABLE C·4 *Value of imports (billions of US dollars)*

	1960	*1970*	*1980*
Major oil-exporting countries	2.070	2.922	25.946
Non-oil-exporting countries	3.837	8.030	34.652
Developing Africa	5.907	10.953	60.598

SOURCE ECA, *Silver Jubilee Meetings,* April–May 1983, p. 27.

TABLE C·5 *Balance of trade (billions of US dollars)*

	1960	*1970*	*1980*
Major oil-exporting countries	−1.143	1.799	37.913
Non-oil-exporting countries	0.128	−0.050	−8.865
Developing Africa	−1.015	1.749	29.048

SOURCE ECA, *Silver Jubilee Meetings,* April–May 1983, p. 27.

TABLE C·6 *Terms of trade (1975=100)*

	1970	*1975*	*1978*	*1979*	*1980*
Oil-exporting countries[a]	34	100	98	115	170
Non-oil-exporting countries	117	100	101	101	113
Developing Africa	65	100	99	110	147
	Purchasing power of exports (1975=100)				
Oil-exporting countries[a]	51	100	118	144	188
Non-oil-exporting countries	109	100	110	117	108
Developing Africa	79	100	114	135	152

[a] Excluding Gabon

SOURCE ECA, *Silver Jubilee Meetings,* April–May 1983, p. 30.

outmoded prognoses and prescriptions: to aspire to a 'willed future' of self-reliance and self-sustainment.[14] Yet the inheritance of incorporation and the impact of recession are uneven, complicating the task of analysis and response.

Indeed, one feature of the *Lagos Plan* and one factor in preparing this study was that of *variability* in political economy, development strategy, and projected future. Paradoxically, while pan-African scholars and pan-African scenarios are maturing in the direction of a consensual paradigm, the country and class relations which they are treating are increasingly divergent: the dialectic between reality and strategy or ideology. Hence the imperative of both sophisticated analysis and sensitive policy as symbolised by the *Plan* itself. For as a report on its implementation recognises:

> [There] are at present 50 member states which, because of various factors (availability of natural resources and high-level skills, access to aid and technical assistance and the zeal with which governments have pursued development and economic growth policies in the past) are at different levels of development and face different types of problems. The result is that different parts of the guidelines will apply to different countries.[15]

African politics, economics and international relations are characterised, then, by expanding, probably exponential, differentiation and divergence. Belatedly, analysis as well as policy has begun to take account of these; hence the trend towards 'political economy' as mode of explanation and of prescription. Even if the continent is still affected substantially by external economic, social and technological changes it may yet be able to escape from external intellectual and policy pressures. As Adedeji insists (and as noted previously in the introduction), the predecessors of the *Lagos Plan* were essential steps in this development of a more indigenous intellectual and analytical framework and formulation – prerequisites for a more autonomous political economy, development strategy and attractive future:

> [In] designing an authentically African pattern of development and life style we have, since the *Revised Framework,* been trying to ensure that it is within the framework of the following six basic conceptual and strategic pillars: national self-reliance and self-sustaining development; democratisation of the development

process; de-alienation; the creation of favourable political and social environment; the recovery of self-confidence by the peoples of Africa in themselves; and, the willingness to achieve an increasing measure of collective self-reliance.[16]

TOWARDS AN AUTHENTIC AFRICAN FUTURE?

So, by apparent contrast, or in apparent contradiction, to Africa's depressing economic conditions and projections, with their external content and constraint, the future for the continent's social scientists and policy planners is now rather promising: as already noted, the very intensity of the African crisis has compelled a dramatic reassessment of both mode of analysis and style of prescription. The *Lagos Plan of Action* – its intellectual antecedents and implementative actions – was not prepared in a vacuum of international conferences and consultants. Rather it emerged out of a period of political and economic re-evaluation as well as depression.

The psychological as well as policy rejuvenation which the *Lagos Plan* engendered at the level of governance – hence the ability and will to mount a determined rejection of the alternative (subversive?) World Bank *Agenda*[17] – serves to reinforce the parallel adoption of more critical modes of analysis at the level of inquiry. If the Pearson Commission represented the embodiment of modernisation ideas and the Brandt Commission those of international developmentalism, then the *Lagos Plan* reflected the popularisation of political economy as well as self-reliant values. Not that these are particularly radical let alone materialist in character – for example, women but not workers are treated in the *Plan*[18] – but they are more compatible with an indigenous anti-*dependentista* tradition than with the inherited and imported developmentalist school.

In short, the African economic crisis has generated at least a conjuncture of modes of investigation and prescription even if it has yet to produce antagonistic contradictions and subsequent syntheses at the level of production. Of course, if the policy redirections are appropriate then some of these anticipated contradictions within and between classes may be mitigated or moderated: the hope of social democrats for a 'willed future'. Conversely, rather than positive syntheses, such redirections may throw up repressive responses which contain their impact: fascist tendencies rather than socialist experiments seem to characterise Africa in the eighties, by contrast to the sixties or seventies.

In any event, although Africa's economic (and strategic) future may remain problematic, its intellectual and political predicament has improved considerably as political economy has been popularised in terms of analysis and *praxis*. The sociology of debates about and designs for the *Lagos Plan* would make for an interesting study of its own.[19] In conclusion, however, although the existential projections remain pessimistic, the political dimension, at least at the pan-African level, is considerably more optimistic. Indeed, the latter reconsideration would probably not have occurred without the former challenge. Any move towards liberation in Namibia and South Africa is likely to reinforce such a trend towards self-reliant development based on critical analysis of the alternative: a continuous tendency towards impoverishment and differentiation. Global structural changes and cycles have, then, reinforced national difficulties and dilemmas, leading to more open-mindedness about development options.

As just indicated, this study was stimulated in part by an attempt to describe and explain variance in African political economies. Ironically, such variance between classes as well as countries lies at the heart of new approaches – an African paradigm? – to analysis and *praxis:* how to minimise antagonisms between and within states at least until such contradictions can be channelled into productive directions. That they have already been so, at least in terms of intellectual activity, augurs well for further dialectical interaction among classes, countries and institutions: out of the continental crisis may yet emerge an African renaissance in culture and society as well as in political economy and technology. If plans proceed towards an African Common Market during the 1990s then that decade, like that of the 1960s, may belong to Africa. As of now, however, the tendency is towards regression rather than progress. As the ECA's Executive Secretary laments, movement is away from rather than towards the *Strategy* and *Plan:*

> Africa's economic situation has continued to deteriorate since their adoption . . . Africa [faces] six devastating and debilitating crises. These are (i) chronic food deficits; (ii) pernicious droughts which are spreading throughout the continent; (iii) high costs of imported energy; (iv) deteriorating terms of trade with the consequential balance of payments deficits; (v) mounting external debts; and (vi) poor economic management. The worsening economic conditions in Africa have remained unabated.[20]

To be sure, this pattern of recession and regression has been uneven, and will continue to be so as oil, commodity and industrial prices fluctuate along with exchange rates (see Tables C·1 and C·6). Nevertheless, the articulation and acceptance of an African paradigm – a consensual, continental approach to processes and policies of political economy – at least offers hope of designing alternative strategies to overcome economic difficulties as well as academic challenges.[21]

The balance or tension between promising prescriptions and depressing projections offers a stark contrast, as Adedeji recognises himself. Economic decolonisation remains a distant dream besides the everyday reality of economic dependence:

> No doubt, there are heights that the African economy will not have been able to reach by 2008 even after a relentless pursuit of the goals of economic decolonisation . . . this willed future based on the *Strategy* and the *Plan* . . . will (not) be an El Dorado. But it will certainly be a much better qualitative and material life than is promised by the historical trends scenario based on the continuation of the colonial and neo-colonial economic policy . . . the . . . *Strategy* and the *Lagos Plan* . . . provide a basis for making a planned but nevertheless complete break with our undignified past . . . they provide also an opportunity for willing for ourselves a dignified future.[22]

Notes and References

INTRODUCTION

1. See Ali A. Mazrui, *The African Condition: A Political Diagnosis* (London: Heineman, 1980).
2. Adebayo Adedeji, 'Africa: The Crisis of Development and the Challenge of a New Economic Order, Address to the Fourth Meeting of the Conference of Ministers and Thirteenth Session of the ECA, Kinshasa, February–March 1977' (Addis Ababa: ECA, 1977) pp. 8 and 10.
3. See Richard A. Higgott, 'From Modernisation Theory to Public Policy: Continuity and Change in the Political Science of Political Development', *Studies in Comparative International Development* 15(4), Winter 1980, pp. 26–58; and Bjorn Beckman 'Political Science and Political Economy', in Yolamu Barongo (ed.), *Political Science in Africa: A Critical Review* (London: Zed, 1983) pp. 101–111.
4. Contrast, for instance, James S. Coleman, 'The Politics of sub-Saharan Africa'; and 'Conclusion: The Political Systems of the Developing Areas', in Gabriel A. Almond & James S. Coleman, *The Politics of Developing Areas* (Princeton: Princeton University Press, 1960) pp. 247–368 and 532–76 with Samir Amin, *Neo-colonialism in West Africa* (Harmondsworth: Penguin, 1973); and *Accumulation on a World Scale: A Critique of the Theory Of Underdevelopment* (New York: Monthly Review, 1974).
5. For one comparison of these documents and debates over them see Timothy M. Shaw, 'Debates About Africa's Future: The Brandt, World Bank, and Lagos Plan blueprints', *Third World Quarterly* 5(2), April 1983, pp. 330–44.
6. Adedeji, 'Africa' p. 19. For more on a new pedagogy as well as a programme for Africa see Albert Trevoedjre, 'Africa Towards the Year 2000: Final Report on the Joint OAU/ECA Symposium on the Future Development of Africa', Appendix C, in Timothy M. Shaw (ed.), *Alternative Futures for Africa* (Boulder: Westview, 1982) pp. 329–40; and OAU, *What Kind of Africa by the Year 2000? Final Report on the Monrovia Symposium* (Geneva: International Institute for Labour Studies for OAU, 1979).
7. For an analogous attempt to do this in the field of African international relations see Timothy M. Shaw, 'Introduction: Towards a Political Economy of African Foreign Policy', in Timothy M. Shaw & Olajide Aluko (eds), *The Political Economy of African Foreign Policy: Comparative Analyses* (Aldershot: Gower, and New York: St Martin's, 1984) pp. 1–24; and *Towards an International Political Economy for the 1980s:*

From Dependence to (inter)Dependence (Halifax: Centre for Foreign Policy Studies, 1983).

8. Issa G. Shivji, 'The State in the Dominated Social Formations of Africa: Some Theoretical Issues', *International Social Sciences Journal* 32(4), 1980, p. 740. See also Peter Waterman, 'On Radicalism in African Studies', in Peter C. W. Gutkind & Peter Waterman (eds), *African Social Studies: A Radical Reader* (London: Heinemann, 1977) pp. 1–17.
9. For preliminary attempts to do this see Timothy M. Shaw, 'Class, Country and Corporation: Africa in the Capitalist World System', in Donald I. Ray *et al.* (eds), *Into the 1980s: Proceedings of the 11th Annual Conference of the Canadian Association of African Studies, Volume 2* (Vancouver: Tantalus, 1981) pp. 19–37; and 'Africa in the World System: Towards More Uneven Development?', in Timothy M. Shaw & 'Sola Ojo (eds), *Africa and the International Political System* (Washington: University Press of America, 1982) pp. 104–36.
10. Aidan Foster-Carter, 'Neo-Marxist Approaches to Development and Underdevelopment', in Emmanuel de Kadt & Gavin Williams (eds), *Sociology and Development* (London: Tavistock, 1974) p. 87. See also Chris Allen & Gavin Williams (eds), *Sub-Saharan Africa* (New York: Monthly Review, 1983); and Bernard Magubane & Nzongola-Ntalaja (eds), *Proletarianisation and Class Struggle in Africa* (San Francisco: Contemporary Marxism, 1983. Number 6).
11. Henrik Secher Marcussen & Jens Erik Torp, *Internationalisation of Capital: Prospects for the Third World. A Re-examination of Dependency Theory* (London: Zed, 1982) p. 159.
12. For critiques of these see Timothy M. Shaw, 'The Political Economy of African International Relations', *Issue* 5(4), Winter 1975, pp. 29–38; and, with Malcolm J. Grieve, 'Dependence or Development: A Review Article on International and Internal Inequalities in Africa', *Development and Change* 8(3), July 1977, pp. 377–408.
13. For an overview of these changes see Timothy M. Shaw, *Towards an International Political Economy for the 1980s: From Dependence to (inter) Dependence* (Halifax: Centre for Foreign Policy Studies, 1983).
14. For an attempt to examine Africa's international relations over several decades see Timothy M. Shaw, 'The Actors in African International Politics', in Timothy M. Shaw & Kenneth A. Heard (eds), *The Politics of Africa: Dependence and Development* (London: Longman, 1979) pp. 357–96.
15. Nigel Harris, *Of Bread and Guns: The World Economy in Crisis* (Harmondsworth: Pelican, 1983) p. 18.
16. See Timothy M. Shaw, 'Non-Aligned States and the New International Economic Order', in Herb Addo (ed.), *Transforming the World Economy? Critical Essays on the NIEO* (London: Hodder & Stoughton, 1984).
17. Jack N. Barkenbus, 'Slowed Economic Growth and Third World Welfare', in Dennis Clark Pirages (ed.), *The Sustainable Society* (New York: Praeger, 1977) pp. 317 and 315.
18. Basil Davidson, *Africa in Modern History: The Search for a New Society* (Harmondsworth: Pelican, 1978) p. 131.

19. For an overview of this scenario see Timothy M. Shaw, 'The Future of the Great Powers in Africa: Towards a Political Economy in Intervention', *Conference on the Great Powers and Africa,* University of Ife, June 1983.
20. Philippe Lemaitre, 'Who Will Rule Africa by the Year 2000?', in Helen Kitchen (ed.), *Africa: From Mystery to Maze* (Lexington: Lexington, 1976. Critical Choices for Americans, Volume 11) p. 270.
21. I. William Zartman, 'Africa', in James N. Rosenau *et al., World Politics: An Introduction* (New York: Free Press, 1976) p. 593.
22. On corporatism on the continent see Timothy M. Shaw, 'Beyond Neocolonialism: Varieties of Corporatism in Africa', *Journal of Modern African Studies* 20(2), June 1982, pp. 239–61.
23. See the range of case studies in Shaw & Aluko (eds), *The Political Economy of African Foreign Policy,* passim.
24. See Shaw (ed.), *Alternative Futures for Africa.*
25. See Timothy M. Shaw, 'OAU: The Forgotten Economic Debate', *West Africa* 3375, 12 April 1982, pp. 983–4; and 'Agenda for Action: Valuable Criticism', *West Africa,* 3377, 26 April 1982, pp. 1131–3. See also papers presented at, 'Lagos Plan of Action Workshop', Centre for African Studies, Dalhousie University, October 1983.
26. Adebayo Adedeji, 'Development and Economic Growth in Africa to the Year 2000: Alternative Projections and Policies', in Shaw (ed.), *Alternative Futures for Africa* pp. 280–1.
27. Ibid, p. 295.
28. See *ECA and Africa's Development 1983–2008* (Addis Ababa: ECA, 1983).
29. See Shaw, 'Africa in the World System', and 'From Dependence to Self-reliance: Africa's Prospects for the Next Twenty Years', *International Journal* 35(4), Autumn 1980, pp. 821–44.
30. Steven Langdon & Lynn K. Mytelka, 'Africa in the Changing World Economy', in Colin Legum *et al., Africa in the 1980s: A Continent in Crisis* (New York: McGraw-Hill for Council on Foreign Relations 1980s Project, 1979) p. 211.
31. For an earlier attempt to relate projections to policy and psychology see Timothy M. Shaw, 'Introduction: The Political Economy in Africa's Futures', in Shaw (ed.), *Alternative Futures for Africa* pp. 1–16. See also Timothy M. Shaw & Olajide Aluko (eds), *Africa Projected: From Recession to Renaissance by the Year 2000?* (London: Macmillan, 1984).
32. John Saul, *The State and Revolution in Eastern Africa* (New York: Monthly Review, 1979) pp. 384–5.
33. Immanuel Wallerstein, *The Capitalist World-Economy* (Cambridge: Cambridge University Press, 1979) p. 67.

1 PROBLEMATIQUE: THE STATE OF THE STATE

1. Foster-Carter, 'Neo-Marxist Approaches to Development and Underdevelopment', p. 81.
2. London: Longman, 1981.

3. See Coleman, 'The Politics of sub-Saharan Africa', pp. 286–7.
4. See Coleman, 'Conclusion: The Political Systems of the Developing Areas', pp. 536–44.
5. See ibid, pp. 562–76.
6. See James S. Coleman & Carl G. Rosberg, 'Introduction', in their collection on *Political Parties and National Integration in Tropical Africa* (Berkeley: University of California Press, 1970).
7. See Robert H. Jackson & Carl G. Rosberg, *Personal Rule in Black Africa: Prince, Autocrat, Prophet, Tyrant* (Berkeley: University of California Press, 1982).
8. See ibid, pp. 1–82.
9. Ibid pp. 22 and 267–70.
10. Vernon McKay (ed.), *African Diplomacy: Studies in the Determinants of Foreign Policy* (New York: Praeger, 1966) p. 22. For a review of such typologies see Timothy M. Shaw & Paul Goulding, 'Alternative Scenarios for Africa', in Shaw (ed.), *Alternative Futures for Africa* pp. 93–105.
11. Immanuel Wallerstein, 'Class and Class Conflict in Africa', *Monthly Review* 26(9), February 1975, p. 35.
12. Samir Amin, *Accumulation on a World Scale: A Critique of the Theory of Underdevelopment, Second Volume* (New York: Monthly Review, 1974) p. 360.
13. See Samir Amin, 'Underdevelopment and Dependence in Black Africa: Origins and Contemporary Forms', *Journal of Modern African Studies* 10(4), December 1972, pp. 509–18.
14. Amin, *Accumulation on a World Scale* p. 372.
15. For one sophisticated attempt to undertake a neo-Marxist analysis of a quintessential 'pluralist' system see Okwudiba Nnoli, *Ethnic Politics in Nigeria* (Enugu: Fourth Dimension, 1978).
16. Ian Roxborough, *Theories of Underdevelopment* (London: Macmillan, 1979) pp. 72 and 73.
17. Amin, *Accumulation on a World Scale* p. 377.
18. Ibid, p. 373.
19. Issa G. Shivji, 'The State in the Dominated Social Formations of Africa: Some Theoretical Issues', *International Social Science Journal* 32(4), 1980, p. 740.
20. Foster-Carter, 'Neo-Marxist Approaches to Development and Underdevelopment'.
21. Shivji, 'The State in the Dominated Social Formations of Africa', p. 740.
22. Amin, *Accumulation on a World Scale* p. 379.
23. James F. Petras *et al. Class, State and Power in the Third World, with Case Studies in Class Conflict in Latin America* (London: Zed, 1984) p. 17.
24. Robert Brenner, 'The Origins of Capitalist Development: A Critique of Neo-Smithian Marxism' *New Left Review* 104, July–August 1977.
25. Shivji, 'The State in the Dominated Social Formations of Africa', p. 740.
26. Petras *et al. Class, State and Power in the Third World* p. 37.
27. Ibid p. xiii.
28. Ibid, p. 39.

29. Immanuel Wallerstein, *The Capitalist World-Economy* (Cambridge: Cambridge University Press, 1979) pp. 117–18.
30. Krishan Kumar, 'The Industrialising and the "Post-Industrial" Worlds: On Development and Futurology', in Emmanuel de Kadt & Gavin Williams (eds), *Sociology and Development* (London: Tavistock, 1974) p. 348.
31. See Shaw, 'The Future of the Great Powers in Africa'.
32. Reprinted in Giovanni Arrighi and John S. Saul, *Essays on the Political Economy of Africa* (New York: Monthly Review, 1973) pp. 336–77.
33. London: Heinemann, 1976. Cf. his latest attempt to apply a distinctive Marxist mode to contemporary Uganda: *Imperialism and Fascism in Uganda* (London: Heinemann, 1983).
34. Cambridge: Schenkman, 1975.
35. *Can Africa Survive? Arguments Against Growth Without Development* (Boston: Little. Brown, 1974).
36. Harmondsworth: Pelican, 1978.
37. Englewood Cliffs: Prentice-Hall, 1977.
38. (Forthcoming).
39. (1981).
40. Yolamu Barongo, 'Alternative Approaches to African Politics', in his collection on *Political Science in Africa* pp. 145 and 151.

2 PROGNOSIS: CONTRADICTIONS AND COALITIONS

1. See the late Thomas Hodgkin's classic study of *Nationalism in Colonial Africa* (New York: New York University Press, 1957).
2. Richard L. Harris, 'The Political Economy of Africa: Underdevelopment or Revolution', in his collection on *The Political Economy of Africa* (Cambridge: Schenkman, 1975) p. 19.
3. Ibid p. 21.
4. Arrighi & Saul, *Essays on the Political Economy of Africa* p. 21.
5. Ibid, p. 45.
6. Cf. the discussion in Harris, 'The Political Economy of Africa', on 'lumpen-ness' (pp. 23–28).
7. See Shaw, 'Beyond Neocolonialism'.
8. Jack Woddis, 'Is There an African National Bourgeoisie?', in Gutkind & Waterman (eds), *African Social Studies* p. 273.
9. Harris, 'The Political Economy of Africa', p. 24.
10. Woddis, 'Is There an African National Bourgeoisie?', p. 272.
11. Ibid.
12. Evans, *Dependent Development* p. 100.
13. Ibid, p. 313.
14. See Timothy M. Shaw, 'Nigeria's Political Economy: Constitutions, Capitalism and Contradictions', *ODI Review* 2, 1980, pp. 76–85.
15. Evans, *Dependent Development* p. 312. On the application of this perspective to the Nigerian case see Timothy M. Shaw, 'Nigeria in the International System', in I. William Zartman (ed.), *The Political Economy of Nigeria* (New York: Praeger, 1983) pp. 207–36.

16. Evans, *Dependent Development* p. 52.
17. Arrighi & Saul, *Essays on the Political Economy of Africa* p. 129.
18. For a general discussion see Nicole Ball, 'The Military in Politics: Who Benefits and How', *World Development* 9(16), June 1981, pp. 569–82.
19. Saul, *The State and Revolution in Eastern Africa* p. 360.
20. See Michael F. Lofchie, 'The Uganda Coup – Class Action by the Military', *Journal of Modern African Studies* 10(1), May 1972, pp. 19–35.
21. Saul, *The State and Revolution in Eastern Africa* p. 351.
22. Ibid p. 350.
23. See Richard Sandbrook & Robin Cohen (eds), *The Development of an African Working Class* (Toronto: University of Toronto Press, 1975).
24. Arrighi & Saul, *Essays on the Political Economy of Africa* p. 141.
25. Ibid, p. 359.
26. On differentiation in the rural areas see Harris, 'The Political Economy of Africa', pp. 28–29.
27. Arrighi & Saul, *Essays on the Political Economy of Africa* p. 409.
28. Hyden, *Beyond Ujamaa in Tanzania* p. 9.
29. Ibid, p. 31.
30. Arrighi & Saul, *Essays on the Political Economy of Africa* p. 409.
31. Ibid, p. 27.
32. Shivji, 'The State in the Dominated Social Formations of Africa', p. 740.
33. See Mai Palmberg (ed.), *Problems of Socialist Orientation in Africa* (Stockholm: Almqvist & Wiksell, 1978).
34. See in particular Saul's work on Tanzania, the assumptions of which are spelled out in his vigorous debate with Cran Pratt in John S. Saul, 'Tanzania's Transition to Socialism', *Canadian Journal of African Studies* 11(2), 1977, pp. 313–39.
35. See D. Wadada Nabudere, *Essays on the Theory and Practice of Imperialism* (London: Onyx, 1979).
36. See William Tordoff & Ali A. Mazrui, 'The Left and the Super-left in Tanzania', *Journal of Modern African Studies* 10(3), October 1972, pp. 427–45.
37. Saul, *State and Revolution in Eastern Africa* p. 361.
38. Richard L. Sklar, 'The Nature of Class Domination in Africa', *Journal of Modern African Studies* 17(4), December 1979, p. 550.
39. Hamza Alavi, 'The State in Post-Colonial Societies: Pakistan and Bangladesh', in Harry Goulbourne (ed.), *Politics and State in the Third World* (London: Macmillan, 1979) p. 41.

3 PROSPECTIVE: MINIMAL GROWTH AND UNEVEN DEVELOPMENT

1. For an introduction to this see Richard A. Higgott, 'Africa, the New International Division of Labour and the Corporate State', *International Studies Association,* Mexico, April 1983; to appear along with other relevant analyses in John Ravenhill (ed.), *Africa in Economic Crisis: Problems and Strategies* (London: Macmillan, 1984).
2. For an overview of such trends see Timothy M. Shaw, 'Beyond

Underdevelopment: The Anarchic State in Africa', *African Studies Association,* Washington, October 1983.

3. See, *inter alia,* Samir Amin *et al., Dynamics of Global Crisis* (London: Macmillan, 1982); and Andre Gunder Frank, *Crisis: In the World Economy* (London: Heinemann, 1980).
4. See Timothy M. Shaw & Orobola Fasehun, 'Varieties of Neo-Colonialism in Africa: Uneven Dependence and Underdevelopment', in Anirudha Gupta (ed.), *Studies in African History and Politics* (New Delhi: Chand, 1984).
5. For an overview of successive leadership generations in Africa from an orthodox perspective see I. William Zartman, 'Social and Political Trends in Africa in the 1980s', in Legum *et al., Africa in the 1980s* pp. 85–91.
6. On the redefinition of 'security' in Africa given both inter-class contradictions and inter-country competition in a post-growth and post-detente period see Robin Luckham, 'Regional security and disarmament in Africa', *Alternatives* 9(1), Spring/Summer 1983; and Timothy M. Shaw, 'Unconventional Conflict in Africa: Nuclear, Class and Guerrilla Struggles, Past, Present and Prospective', *Jerusalem Journal of International Relations* (forthcoming).
7. For an informed insight to the politics of decay in this case see Naomi H. Chazan, *An Anatomy of Ghanaian Politics: Managing Political Recession, 1969–1982* (Boulder: Westview, 1983).
8. For a useful overview of informal sectors and 'unofficial' development, particularly in West Africa, see Richard Sandbrook, *The Politics of Basic Needs: Urban Aspects of Assaulting Poverty in Africa* (Toronto: University of Toronto Press, 1982), passim.
9. For a general introduction to this set of relations and assumptions as well as to the Zambian case, see Jane L. Parpart, *Labour and Capital on the African Copperbelt* (Philadelphia: Temple University Press, 1983).
10. See Shaw & Fasehun, 'Varieties of Neocolonialism in Africa'.
11. See Timothy M. Shaw, 'Beyond Neocolonialism: Varieties of Corporatism in Africa', *Journal of Modern African Studies* 20(2), June 1982, pp. 239–61. For the World Bank lament, from a very different perspective, about excessive bureaucratisation see *World Development Report 1983,* especially pp. 4–127.
12. On the Nigerian case, including President Shagari's call for an 'ethical' as well as 'green' revolution, see Julius O. Ihonvbere & Timothy M. Shaw, 'Nigeria: Oil Production, Class Formation and Social Contradictions in a (semi-)Peripheral Capitalist Society', *Canadian Association of African Studies* Quebec, May 1983.
13. For a welcome discussion and dissection of 'populism' see Gavin Kitching, *Development and Underdevelopment in Historical Perspective: Populism, Nationalism and Industrialisation* (London: Methuen, 1982), passim.
14. See Timothy M. Shaw, 'Reviews', in *ODI Review* 2, 1980, pp. 76–85; and *ODI Review* 2, 1982, pp. 72–5.
15. Samir Amin, *Neo-Colonialism in West Africa* (Harmondsworth: Pelican, 1983) p. 226.

16. See Peter Evans, *Dependent Development: The Alliance of Multinational, State and Local Capital in Brazil* (Princeton: Princeton University Press, 1979), pp. 11–12 and 274–329.
17. See Simon Jenkins, 'Destabilisation in Southern Africa', *The Economist* 288 (7298), pp. 16–22, July 1983, pp. 15–28; and Timothy M. Shaw, 'Dilemmas of Dependence and (under) Development: Conflicts and Choices in Zambia's Present and Prospective Foreign Policy', *Africa Today* 26(4), Fourth Quarter 1979, pp. 43–65; and 'The Political Economy of Zambia', *Current History* 81(473), March 1982, pp. 125–8 and 144.
18. See Shaw, 'Nigeria in the International System', in Zartman (ed.), *The Political Economy of Nigeria,* pp. 207–36.
19. For critical overviews of these in selected cases from both periphery and semi-periphery see Shaw & Aluko (eds), *The Political Economy of African Foreign Policy*.
20. See, for example, Jane L. Parpart & Timothy M. Shaw, 'Cycles, Contradictions and Coalitions: Class Fractions in Zambia, 1964–1984', in Irving L. Markovitz (ed.), *Studies in Power and Class in Africa* (forthcoming).
21. On such divisions in the case of Canadian interests concerned with foreign policy see Cranford Pratt, 'Canadian Foreign Policy: Bias to Business', *International Perspectives,* November/December 1982, pp. 3–6; and Robert O. Matthews, 'The Churches and Foreign Policy', *International Perspectives* January/February 1983, pp. 18–21.
22. For two revealing yet symptomatic cases see Steven W. Langdon, 'Industrial Dependence and Export Manufacturing in Kenya'; and Lynn K. Mytelka, 'Direct Foreign Investment and Technological Choice in the Ivorian Textile and Wood Industries', in Ravenhill (ed.), *Africa in Economic Crisis.*
23. Harris, *Of Bread and Guns,* p. 68.
24. *Agenda for Action,* p. 93.
25. See *A Programme for the Industrial Decade for Africa prepared jointly by the ECA, OAU and UNIDO* (Vienna: UNIDO, 1982).
26. See Florizelle B. Liser, 'A Basic Needs Strategy and the Physical Quality of Life Index (PQLI)', in Shaw (ed.), *Alternative Futures for Africa,* pp. 201–36; and with E. Dianne White, 'African Development and the Elusiveness of BHN', in Shaw and Aluko (eds), *Africa Projected.*
27. On this medium-term goal see 'Final Act of Lagos', in *Lagos Plan of Action,* p. 128.
28. This, despite the notice given to Africa's peripheral problems in *North-South: A Programme for Survival* (London: Pan, 1983) pp. 78–9; and *Common Crisis, North-South: Co-operation for World Recovery* (London: Pan, 1983) p. 22.
29. See Frances Stewart, 'Brandt II: The Mirage of Collective Action in a Self-serving World', *Third World Quarterly* 5(3), July 1983, pp. 640–9.
30. See Claude Ake, *Revolutionary Pressures in Africa* (London: Zed, 1978) pp. 92–4.
31. Adebayo Adedeji, 'The Evolution of the Monrovia Strategy and the

Lagos Plan of Action: A Regional Approach to Economic Decolonisation' (Addis Ababa: ECA, 1983) pp. 23–4.

4 PRESCRIPTION: WHAT IS TO BE DONE?

1. See Timothy M. Shaw, 'Introduction: Are the 1980s Characterised by Crisis and or Conjuncture?', in Shaw & Aluko (eds), *Africa Projected.*
2. Basil Davidson, *Africa in Modern History: The Search for a New Society* (Harmondsworth: Pelican, 1978) p. 287.
3. Philippe Lemaitre, 'Who Will Rule Africa by the Year 2000?', in Helen Kitchen (ed.), *Africa: From Mystery to Maze* (Lexington: Lexington, 1976. Critical Choices for Americans, Volume 11) p. 264.
4. Davidson, *Africa in Modern History,* p. 295.
5. Aguibou Yansané, 'Decolonisation, Dependency and Development in Africa: The Theory Revisited', in his collection on *Decolonisation and Dependency: Problems of Development in African Societies* (Westport: Greenwood, 1980) p. 27.
6. Davidson, *Africa in Modern History,* p. 329.
7. See Timothy M. Shaw, 'The Political Economy of African International Relations', *Issue* 5(4), Winter 1975, pp. 29–38; and 'Introduction: Towards a Political Economy of African Foreign Policy', in Shaw & Aluko (eds) *The Political Economy of African Foreign Policy,* pp. 1–24.
8. Davidson, *Africa in Modern History,* p. 376.
9. Lemaitre, 'Who Will Rule Africa by the Year 2000?', p. 266.
10. Thomas Kanza, *Evolution and Revolution in Africa* (Cambridge: Schenkman, 1979) pp. 70–1.
11. Lemaitre, 'Who Will Rule Africa by the Year 2000?', p. 275.
12. Petras *et al., Class, State and Power in the Third World,* p. 38.
13. Cf. Goran Hyden, *Beyond Ujamaa in Tanzania: Underdevelopment and an Uncaptured Peasantry* (London: Heinemann, 1980). See also Shaw, 'Beyond Underdevelopment: The Anarchic State in Africa'.
14. See Mamdani, *Imperialism and Fascism in Uganda.*
15. See Claude E. Welch & Ronald I. Meltzer (eds), *Human Rights and Development in Africa: Domestic, Regional and International Dilemmas* (Albany: SUNY Press, 1984).
16. Reprinted as Appendix One in Ibid.
17. See International Labour Office, *Employment, Growth and Basic Needs: A One-World Problem* (New York: Praeger for ILO and ODC, 1977).
18. Fawzi Mansour, 'Some Notes on Social Stratification and Social Change in Africa: Some Theoretical Considerations', *Africa Development* 3(3), July–September 1978, pp. 11–12.
19. Nicola Swainson, *The Development of Corporate Capitalism in Kenya, 1918–1977* (Berkeley: University of California Press, 1980) p. 14.
20. Roxborough, *Theories of Underdevelopment,* p. 135.
21. For critical overviews of the current state of this debate see Robin Luckham, 'Regional Security and Disarmament in Africa', *Alternatives* (forthcoming); and Timothy M. Shaw, 'Unconventional Conflict in Africa: Nuclear, Class and Guerrilla Struggles, Past, Present and Prospective', *Jerusalem Journal of International Studies* (forthcoming).

22. Samir Amin, *Neo-colonialism in West Africa* (Harmondsworth: Penguin, 1973) p. 226.
23. On such a struggle in Zambia see Shaw & Parpart, 'Cycles, Contradictions and Coalitions: Class Fractions in Zambia, 1964–1984'.
24. See Luckham, 'Regional Security and Disarmament in Africa'; and Shaw, 'Unconventional Conflict in Africa'.
25. Christine A. Bogdanowicz-Bindert, 'Sub-Saharan Africa: An Agenda for Action', *Journal of World Trade Law* 16(4), July–August 1982, p. 283.
26. Ibid, p. 286. For a set of papers and presentations which ended up concurring with such a conclusion see 'Africa: Which Way Out of the Recession?', *Scandinavian Institute of African Studies,* Uppsala, September 1982. A selection of case studies from this conference appeared in Jerker Carlsson (ed.), *Recession in Africa* (Uppsala: Scandinavian Institute of African Studies, 1983).
27. (Geneva: International Institute for Labour Studies, 1981).
28. See Shaw (ed.), *Alternative Futures for Africa.*
29. See Shaw & Aluko (eds), *Africa Projected.*
30. See Claude Ake, *Revolutionary Pressures in Africa* (London: Zed, 1978) pp. 92–4.
31. Adebayo Adedeji, 'Development and Economic Growth in Africa to the Year 2000', in Shaw (ed.), *Alternative Futures for Africa,* p. 281.
32. See Timothy M. Shaw, 'Introduction: Are the 1980s Characterised by Crisis and/or Conjuncture?', in Shaw & Aluko (eds), *Africa Projected.*
33. Adedeji, 'Development and Economic Growth in Africa to the Year 2000', p. 301.
34. See Ali A. Mazrui, *The African Condition* (London: Heinemann, 1980).
35. See World Bank, *Accelerated Development in Sub-Saharan Africa: Agenda for Action* (Washington, 1981).
36. 'Accelerated Development in sub-Saharan Africa: An Assessment by OAU, ECA and ADB Secretariats' (Council of Ministers 38th Ordinary Session, Addis Ababa, 22 February to 1 March 1982. CM 1177 (XXXVIII) Annex 1) p. 29.
37. *Lagos Plan of Action,* p. 5.
38. *Accelerated Development in sub-Saharan Africa,* p. 5.
39. *Lagos Plan of Action,* p. 8.
40. *Accelerated Development in sub-Saharan Africa,* p. 17.
41. OAU, 'Report of the Secretary-General on the World Bank report' (Council of Ministers 38th Ordinary Session, Addis Ababa, 23 February to 1 March 1982, CM/1177 (XXXVIII)) Appendix II, p. 1.
42. See chapter by Langdon, in Ravenhill (ed.), *Africa in Economic Crisis.*
43. See Shaw, 'Beyond Underdevelopment'.
44. See Timothy M. Shaw, 'Beyond Neo-colonialism: Varieties of Corporatism in Africa', *Journal of Modern African Studies* 20(2), June 1982, 239–61.
45. Henrik Secker Marcussen & Jens Erik Torp, *Internationalization of Capital: Prospects for the Third World. A re-examination of Dependency theory* (London: Zed, 1982) pp. 164–5.

46. See Mary Kaldor, *The Disintegrating West* (Harmondsworth: Pelican, 1979).
47. See Shaw, 'Beyond Neo-colonialism', pp. 254–61.
48. Ruth Berins Collier & David Collier, 'Inducement versus Constraints: Disaggregating "corporatism"', *American Political Science Review* 73(4), December 1979, p. 967.
49. Alfred Stepan, *The State and Society: Peru in Comparative Perspective* (Princeton: Princeton University Press, 1978) p. 80.
50. Ravi Gulhati, 'Industrial Strategy for Late Starters: The Experience of Kenya, Tanzania and Zambia', World Bank Staff Working Paper Number 457, Washington, May 1981.
51. Guillermo A. O'Donnell, 'Corporatism and the Question of the State', in James M. Malloy (ed.), *Authoritarianism and Corporatism in Latin America* (Pittsburgh: University of Pittsburgh Press, 1977) p. 78.
52. See Timothy M. Shaw, 'Brandt, Bank and Plan: Debates and Dialectics About Africa's Future', *Third World Quarterly* 5(2), April 1983, pp. 330–44.

CONCLUSION

1. Beckman, 'Political Science and Political Economy', pp. 109 and 110.
2. See Barongo (ed.), *Political Science in Africa,* passim.
3. Adebayo Adedeji, 'The Evolution of the Monrovia Strategy and the Lagos Plan of Action: A Regional Approach to Economic Decolonisation' (Addis Ababa: ECA, 1983) p. 2. See also his useful historical-cum-political-cum-philosophical 'Introduction', in *ECA and Africa's Development, 1983–2008* pp. 1–3.
4. See ECA, *Revised Framework of Principles for the Implementation of the New International Economic Order in Africa, 1976–1981–1986* (Addis Ababa, 1976).
5. Adedeji, 'The Evolution of the Monrovia Strategy and the Lagos Plan of Action', p. 8.
6. For more on the contribution of, and constraints on, the ECA as an innovative, even progressive, institution see Timothy M. Shaw, 'Towards a Political Economy of the Lagos Plan: Innovation, Interest and Ideology', *Lagos Plan of Action Workshop* Centre for African Studies, Dalhousie University, October 1983.
7. Cf. the revisionist modernisation perspective still pervading World Bank thinking – the call for renewed concentration on 'Management in Development' – in *World Development Report 1983* (Washington: OUP for IBRD, 1983) pp. 41–127.
8. See 'A Tribute to Ruth First'; and 'Mpakati Assassination', *Review of African Political Economy* 25, September–December 1982, pp. 3–65; and 'Attati Mpakati – Assassination of a Malawi Revolutionary', *Journal of African Marxists,* 4, September 1983, pp. 103–5.
9. See *inter alia* Ali A. Mazrui, *Africa's International Relations: The Diplomacy of Dependency and Change* (Boulder: Westview, 1977) pp. 29–35.

10. S. Egite Oyovbaire, 'The Tyranny of Borrowed Paradigms and the Responsibility of Political Science: The Nigerian Experience', in Barongo (ed.), *Political Science in Africa,* p. 252.
11. 'Survey: World Economy 1983', *The Economist* 288(7308), 24 September 1983, p. 5.
12. *World Development Report, 1983,* p. 125.
13. Ibid, p. 24.
14. *ECA and Africa's Development 1983–2008,* pp. 2 and 93–6.
15. See 'Implementation of the Lagos Plan of Action' (Addis Ababa: ECA, April 1982. E/CN.14/TPCW/II/18/Rev 2) p. 6.
16. Adedeji, 'The Evolution of the Monrovia Strategy and the Lagos Plan of Action', p. 12. For one attempt to investigate and improve on economic nationalism on the continent see Adebayo Adedeji (ed.), *Indigenization of African Economies* (London: Hutchinson, 1981).
17. See Shaw, 'OAU: Forgotten Economic Debate', and 'The African Crisis: Debates and Dialectics over Alternative Development Strategies for the Continent', *Alternatives* 9(1), Spring/Summer 1983, pp. 111–27.
18. Contrast papers by Jane Parpart & Joseph Engwenyu, respectively, at *Lagos Plan of Action Workshop,* to appear in a collection edited by David Fashole Luke & Timothy M. Shaw in the Dalhousie African Studies Series published by University Press of America. One of the fundamental flaws in the present essay and in much neo-Marxist analysis is the exclusion of gender as a crucial factor in underdevelopment. The intricate relationships of class and sexual divisions of labour are central yet elusive. Clearly different historical periods and distinctive political economies affect the sexual division of labour as well as class antagonisms.
19. The 'official' history has begun to be written by Adedeji in his UN pamphlet on 'The Evolution of the Monrovia Strategy and the Lagos Plan of Action' but an unofficial account, with particular reference to academics' input to the *Revised Framework,* Monrovia consultation and subsequent attempts at popularisation, still awaits an author.
20. Adedeji, 'The Evolution of the Monrovia Strategy and the Lagos Plan of Action', p. 18.
21. See Chapter 1 on the continuing resistance to 'political economy' from Western intellectuals and institutions, notably Jackson & Rosberg, *Personal Rule in Black Africa* and *Agenda for Action,* respectively. The 'management' perspective embodied in *World Development Report 1983* constitutes a non-Marxist form of political economy within the modernisation mould.
22. Adedeji, 'The Evolution of the Monrovia Strategy and the Lagos Plan of Action', pp. 21–2.

Index